The f Word

faith is...

G Ajewole

Publishers
Publish.Market.Sell

For permission request, contact the publisher
at the email address below:
Email: info@sdpublishers.com
Website: www.sdpublishers.com

Author: Gbenga Ajewole
Publisher: SDPublishers

Cover Design: SharpShot Creative
Photography: Jadanna Huie @ Photo Confectionery

Distributed by SDPublishers

Paperback ISBN: 978-1-908386-02-1

Quotations
www.thinkexist.com/quotations/faith
www.quotegarden.com

Dedication

To my beautiful wife Selone, my son Aryeh,
Mum and you the reader -
my fellow Faithllionaire,
this book's raison d'être.

Acknowledgement

First and foremost, I'm eternally grateful to Jesus Christ, my Saviour, my Hero, my King, my Friend and my Inspiration. In Him, I find and walk in my purpose. I'm so glad for the second chance. You took me out of the gutter and gave me a message to share with the world. My faith starts and ends with you.

To my best friend, my soul mate and my queen – Selone, if all wives loved like you, the world would constantly smile. Thank you for believing in me, and releasing me to do what I do! Aryeh, you kept daddy up all night, but watching you grow is a true joy.

A huge thank you to the worlds greatest mum. Thank you for always being a praying mum, loving and praying me into the faith. Your faith and love inspires me. My mum-in-law, thanks for allowing me to be your son. I cherish you.

I want to appreciate my in-laws, cousins and friends; thank you for sharing me with the world.

To my mentor and spiritual father - Chief, your life of service and faith is a true inspiration. Thanks for always believing in me, and allowing me to follow you, as you follow Christ.

I'm indebted to so many amazing young men and women, who have encouraged me, and made this book project a reality.

Abi, thank you for your organizational skills, and pushing me to get up and write. I am indebted to Louisa and Yemi, for giving up many days and nights to go through my many grammatical mishaps and putting things right.

Sotonye at SD Publishers, thank you for performing a miracle, by turning pages of email attachments into a book.

I want to extend my gratitude to the amazing souls at Destiny Christian Fellowship; it is a great joy to pastor such an eclectic, diverse and beautiful family of believers.

To all the staff and volunteers at PGA Ministries, SAGE Ministries, Inspired-4-Purpose and The Rock Church, I appreciate and love you greatly.

Contents

Foreword

'The F Word', authored by Gbenga Ajewole, is a must read. It is brilliant, exciting, enlightening and factual. Pastor G, in very simple and understandable terms, demonstrates the plain truths of biblical faith and shows how to seek, possess and apply it. Indeed, faith is measurable: there's little faith (Matt. 14:31), great faith (Matt. 8:10), growing faith (2 Thess. 1:3), weak faith (Rom. 4:19), strong faith (Rom. 4:20), rich faith (James 2:5), full of faith (Acts 6:5), perfect faith (James 2:22), overcoming faith (1 John 5:4); unfeigned faith (1 Tim. 1:5), shipwrecked faith (1 Tim. 1:19), and so on. The teaching and encouragement that God has brought Gbenga to bear to us through 'The F Word' is that we must continue to aim for the highest level of faith, and to reach for the stars and beyond, because it is obtainable and attainable. Once faith is present, with God all things are possible, whatever the challenges one may be facing. 'The F Word' makes it very clear that, once you have solid faith and you put it into practice, you will achieve worthy results and your end will be better than your beginning. It is a book of great, yet realistic and God ordained, encouragement.

This book is nothing short of an inspired and anointed work, and the author, from my own personal knowledge of, and close association with him over many years, is a man after God's heart, very genuine and sincere, down to earth, humble, diligent, passionate and zealous about the things of God. He has the mind of Christ (Philippians 2:5; Galatians 5:22-23), and I am therefore not surprised that God has used him to anchor this laudable project which I would boldly and confidently, for the quality it oozes on its every page, recommend the reader to utilise regularly as a Bible companion. The book is a beautiful read, it holds one's attention, is so interesting, revealing and obviously practical that, once you start to read it, it becomes 'unputdownable' -you want to read it over and over again. It's certainly a gripping piece. The book, like its author, is very positive and full of light from beginning to end.

'The F Word' is devoid of quantity (i.e verbosity) -it is a short work, but it is full of quality, and its structure and content are simple, yet profound, powerful and compelling. The author models great endurance and is clearly a man who lives by genuine faith in God with Jesus as his Lord and Saviour, and all he submits in this book are a true and honest reflection of how he lives his life. This unique and gifted man's antecedents make 'The F Word' a worthwhile read. This book will assure you that God indeed makes miracles out of faith and that, in all the setbacks of your life as a believer, God is plotting for your joy. I, without any reservation whatsoever, again recommend this book to you and everyone, to read, digest and treasure.

Kolade 'Chief' Adebayo-Oke, Pastor

One of the most mysterious, evading and often misunderstood realities in the human experience is the reality of faith. It is the one thing that the Scripture states the lack thereof keeps us from pleasing the Creator thus disqualifying us from the awesome future He longs to create for His people. In Pastor G's groundbreaking book "The F-Word", the realities of faith are unpacked and unveiled with much practicality allowing the reader to both develop and utilize their faith-muscle to bring into manifestation the things that they've hoped for. Whether you are new to the subject of faith or looking to increase your measure for greater results in your life this book is sure to accelerate your success and elevate your joy.

-Touré Roberts – Entrepreneur, Producer, Pastor, Mentor to the stars!

This is a truly inspirational book about the most important aspect of our relationship with God, faith. It does a lot in highlighting the different aspects of faith that one takes for granted once one decides to follow Christ. I particularly found the section about the growth and stickiness of faith most encouraging because sometimes we pray for everything else but an increase in faith. We sometimes take it for granted that we have faith. The language and tone of the text is also really helpful as we are given real life examples and anecdotes that are easily digestible. It is an exciting book that will have mainstream appeal

- Femi Oyeniran - Actor

The F word...Wow! Wow! Wow!
All I can say is thank you Lord for divine connections. This book is truly refreshing!

At my first meeting with Pastor G, I perceived very quickly that this man of God was unique, different and simply a nice down to earth kind of guy. His ability to connect with the younger generation, whilst still keeping it Kingdom and real, truly blesses me.

From the onset, I was totally intrigued by the title Pastor G had given to this book. So with my mind running in all directions, trying to figure out what exactly the 'F' word could possibly stand for, I was quite relieved to find out that he was still on the right track to heaven. If, like me, you have picked up this book simply because you were intrigued by the title, I have great news for you: you will not be disappointed at all. As you delve deeper into these well presented chapters, not only will you get to encounter the authentic character and personality of Pastor G, I promise, you will be totally inspired and stirred into onward movement. The F Word aims to answer and clear up any questions, doubts, mindsets, myths and confusions you may have on the subject of 'Faith', in a simple, yet totally effective way. Pastor G has been blessed with a God given gift to relate to both the young and old alike, and there is something for everyone within the pages of this book. If you are simply looking to start, renew, develop or exercise your faith walk, trust me, 'The F Word' is a must read.

- Sasha D Taylor - Author 'Broken but I'm healed

Very inspirational book with practical and direct answers to the question, what is faith? I was so blessed and inspired reading Pastor G's deep, but practical insight on how to live by faith. This book will help you understand how to rise above fear in your everyday life. With the inspiration given to him by the Spirit of God and by his life experiences, Pastor G has giving us a book that will bless many. If you have ever asked yourself, "How can I share what I believe with someone else?", this book is for you.

- Jason Jackson - Pastor & Social Entrepreneur

I have known Pastor G Ajewole for over 20 years, and I believe wholeheartedly that this poignant book should be in the hands of everyone. This great book accentuates the profound proclivities of people from all walks of life. And gives hope, faith and assurance that we can win in the game of life by the 'F' word through the vicissitudes of what I call the game of L.I.F.E (Living In Full Excellence).

As a new generation leader Pastor G Ajewole delivers us a masterpiece not just to the new generation but also to the generations to come! Which is contextualized in a way made relevant to a needy world to reinforce the power of the 'F' word - FAITH.

- Pastor Dr. TWS Johnson - Excel Centre International

G's excellent use of imagery, personal experience and humour allows you to see faith in a different light! Definitely a book for all!

- Emmanuel Akintunde - Actor

Pastor G's F Word is a positive, energising piece of work that combines the idea of old fashioned belief in a greater power alongside personal, real anecdotes and thoughts about faith by a man that has lived both sides of the road. The chapters and words juxtapose the idea of faith and enable the reader to understand the concept in a logical, clarified way. By using real, current topical subjects and ideas, Pastor G manages to make faith attainable and breaks down any cynical disbelief and turns it into belief with simple, easily understandable concepts in the greater good to inspire the reader to be the best that they can be. - a lesson he has lived, learnt and now passes on. In a world where many are overwhelmed and lost, the F Word brings us back to a neutral positive understanding. A must have bedside table book to reach across to time and again.

- Jasmine Dotiwala – TV Presenter

Introduction

"Faith is knowing and actively believing (with related action) that there will be a light at the end of the tunnel." – G Ajewole

A few years ago my wife and I made the long hop across the pond to New York. Whilst in Times Square I came across the now infamous 'Got Milk?' advertising campaigns plastered across giant billboards. I knew that milk was imperative for our growth, and the various adverts always rightly depicted the benefits of drinking milk. The imagery used on the adverts were of famous athletes, models, actors and other celebrity-types, almost suggesting that successful and good looking people drink milk. This advert got me thinking what a person with faith looks like.

On the return flight back to London, we experienced a little turbulence, which for me was a big thing. Those close to me know although I love travelling and visiting amazing destinations across the globe, I totally dislike flying, especially long-haul flights. Up to now, I still refuse to sit on the window seat on flights. During the 15 seconds of turbulence, which to me felt more like an eternity, I posed a question to myself, I said 'Self, Got faith?' As a Christian, a ministry leader, a husband, and a man; I knew that I was letting myself down by not practising what I preached. I would always be the one to tell others to have faith, and how our faith is a sensor that is greater than our five natural sensory organs. Yet a little turbulence had caused me to act like a whimpy kid in a playground full of bullies. I made a decision right then to man up, and activate the faith that I believe that I have. At that moment, I realised that the imagery used in the 'Got Milk?' adverts were there to show 'what milk can do', and that as a person of faith, I needed to remind myself 'what faith can do and what faith should be'...

This book is intended to help you, no matter who you are, to explore the concept of faith in an understandable way using basic concepts and everyday language. As a minister of the Gospel, I have a passion to see God's amazing people be all they can be in Him, and fulfil destiny. I understand the need for a strong faith in order to counteract all the negativities we experience, and fight back against the oppositions we encounter on the road to fulfilling our destiny in Christ. I hope that you are able to weave the ideas and 'nuggets' on the pages of this book into your everyday life, and grow in your understanding and application of faith, so that you can be the best YOU, you were created to be. Our Creator has called us to overcome and to live victoriously, we need to be able to see beyond the now, and view life at the 'bigger picture' level. In order to do this effectively and successfully, we need to utilise our faith in Him. Our faith should not be like a piece of Grandma's expensive China, which is left unused for decades on display, kept in a glass cabinet. Rather we need to make sure we put our faith to use every day, every hour, every minute and every second of our lives.

I truly hope that this book inspires, motivates and propels you to explore your faith. I'm excited to be part of your journey towards discovering how potent and powerful your faith can be.

1

Faith is...

"Now faith is being sure of what we hope for and certain of what we do not see" – Hebrews 11:1 (NASB)

How would you complete this sentence? Real Faith is...? As you unveil the first chapter of this book, take a moment to think about what your definition of faith is, how you have interpreted faith, and what you perceive faith to be.

Faith is not what some of us think it is. Oftentimes our human dreaming is a mere delusion, which is often mis-interpreted as faith. Rather, faith is living, it's unshakeable, it's life giving and it's active. Faith in its rawest and undiluted form is a surety and a belief in the certainty of a thing, irrespective of what we see or do not see. Faith is more than positive thinking, more than pop psychology, more than a feeling, and more than our denominational affiliation.

Some people have diminished faith and placed it in a box to mean simply wishful thinking or a mere cocktail of good intentions. The main element in faith is expressed by looking at the original Greek word '*pistis*' which simply translates as 'firm persuasion'. To elaborate on this, according to the Greek expression, to have faith is to have a firm, unshakable persuasion about a thing, an outcome, a future, based on a deeply rooted belief in someone.

Many people, Christians and non-Christians alike, often have a sense of faith, and a hope for something or someone, and that is exactly where the problem lies. Because faith is not based on the thing hoped for, but rather faith is dependent on the object, which that faith is rested upon.

Some of us are familiar with the story of Abraham in Scriptures. Abraham believed when, from a logical and human point of view, there was no basis for hope at all. Abraham and his barren wife were way past childbearing age; as we would say, they were 'over the hill.'

The object of Abraham's faith was God, and in particular the promise that he (Abraham), would become the father of many nations, as he had been told, "So shall your offspring be" (Romans 4:18b). God had called Abraham and spoken to him of the great promise that awaits him in Genesis 12:1-3. After many years, when Abraham still did not have any descendants, God took him outside and said, "Look toward heaven, and number the stars, if you are able to number them." Then He said to him, "So shall your offspring be." (Genesis 15:5) Many of us would find it difficult to take God up on His promises at such a suggestion. Looking at the factors around him, Abraham could have easily chosen to dispel God's promises as simply disillusioned, motivational empty words, but instead, Abraham chose to believe God. The question is do we always make a choice to believe God, when every logical calculation goes against what God has promised?

"And Abraham believed the LORD, and He counted it to him as righteousness" (Genesis 15:6).

The object of real living faith is God! Real faith works because of its object. It is not the amount or sincerity of faith that saves or heals. A person can have a great deal of faith or be extremely sincere in his or her faith, but that is not what brings about breakthrough or the realisation of what is hoped for.

You may have a monstrous amount of faith and be extremely sincere in your faith, believing that if you step off the top of a 25-storey skyscraper (which, by the way I don't suggest you do!), you will reach the ground unharmed. The problem is not the amount or sincerity of your faith but rather with the object of your faith. You believe that the laws of gravity will be changed in order to allow you to float to the ground unharmed. Unfortunately, (unlike the Red Bull adverts suggest) that will not happen.

No, the important thing is that the object of your faith must be placed in the right person – God! Abraham was saved because his faith was in God.

Hebrews chapter 11 is often referred to as the Chapter of faith and the opening verse gives a great insight and correct perspective on what faith is. Biblical faith by definition is 'the substance of things hoped for, the evidence of things not seen.' If faith, therefore, is a substance, that means that it is tangible; a real thing. It is the reality of what you are actually hoping for. Faith is more than mere wishful thinking, it is the reality we choose to believe, hope for, expect, anticipate and ultimately accept.

Hebrews 11 also tells us that faith is evidence. Anyone who is familiar with shows such as CSI, The Bill, Silent Witness, or real life forensic police work, would know that when a crime is committed, clues are pieced together by looking at the evidence available on the scene of the crime or on the suspect. Therefore, in an unconventional way, if faith is the evidence, it simply means that something has already happened in the spiritual realm, and our faith sees this evidence and utilises it as the active engine and the tangible belief until what has already happened in the spiritual now manifests in the natural. To understand faith as an evidence is to take hold of faith as our assurance of the existence of things we cannot see; it galvanizes us to keep on ticking when we've taken a licking in this thing called life, and to keep on going even when the fat lady has sung her last note.

Real faith is a work of God in us which brings about real change in real people. In essence, faith brings about a new birth. Real faith kills off the old you, and unveils a brand new you, a brand new you with a completely new heart, new mind, new senses, new ways of reasoning, new power, new passions and a reliance on the Holy Spirit as our personal satellite navigation system. Faith is truly living, truly creative, truly active, and ever so powerful. Faith always sees a way out and anticipates the positive. Faith is more than what we say, preach or sing about on Sundays... Faith is something that gives us the strength to live, faith is the power to overcome, faith is the spring that enables us to bounce-back from life's setbacks. Faith is a liberator to those of us who have been trapped by fear, anxiety, worry or guilt.

Contrary to some people's religious persuasion or preaching, faith is not measured by our possessions. Some misguided folks have devalued faith to merely basing it upon how many physical or material possessions one has accrued. To have a Bentley, a private jet, a 10 bedroom house, a great job, a diamond presidential Rolex watch (all nice things!) has been believed to mean that one has great faith. I'm of the persuasion that real faith is exercised when one has nothing left apart from a total dependence on God, therefore faith is best expressed when what we expect / await is so far removed from what we see in the physical. Let's remember that faith is the evidence of what we do not see.

Faith is the cornerstone, the bedrock and the engine to everyone and anyone who is alive and believes in possibilities.

'Got faith?'

Great ideas about faith...

"The world tells us that 'seeing is believing', but faith says 'believing is seeing' "–G AJEWOLE

"Faith is a bird that feels dawn breaking and sings while it is still dark." – RABINDRANATH TAGORE

"Faith isn't the ability to believe long and far into the misty future. It's simply taking God at His Word and taking the next step."
– JONI ERICKSON TADA

"The antidote to frustration is a calm faith, not in your own cleverness, or in hard toil, but in God's guidance."
– NORMAN VINCENT PEALE

"Faith is believing in things when common sense tells you not to"
– GEORGE SEATON

My Thoughts

2

Faith is a Weapon

"...take up the shield of faith, with which you can extinguish all the flaming arrows of the evil one" – Ephesians 6:16 (NIV)

In the summer of 2010, I watched a BBC 3 documentary titled 'My dog is a weapon'. This documentary followed the recent trend in young men across London keeping and breeding banned breeds of dogs in order to use them in intimidations, fights and robberies. The young men realised that walking around the streets of London with a gun or knife would result in a VIP long stay at Her Majesty's pleasure if they were caught. Therefore a conventional weapon of choice in a knife or gun was replaced with a dog. No longer did local gangsters or 'rude boys' have the need to walk around the high streets with a knife or gun, but rather the new weapon was a ruthless looking, attack-on-command pit-bull or Staffordshire bull terrier. Watching this documentary gave me the inspiration to look at what I could use to intimidate, fight and corner my enemy – the enemy of my destiny. It was my faith. My faith is a weapon against the enemy.

In this journey of life, every one of us will encounter circumstances, incidents and situations with various degrees of intensity and lengths of time. Oftentimes these encounters leave us depleted, worn out and simply exhausted. Even when all has been stripped away, faith is what is to be used to fight back; it's the believer's counter-terrorism weapon of choice against the terrorist of our destiny and wiles of the enemy.

John 10:10 reminds us that the enemy has three basic agendas; to kill us of all our joy, to steal away our identity and destroy our hope in the assured victory we have been afforded in Christ Jesus. Many of us at some point, especially when life seems to be squeezing the very wind out of us, seem to surrender to the enemy's agenda; we second guess who we are in Christ, we second guess our value, we question God's love for us, we doubt our promised future (Jeremiah 29:11), we are consumed with fear, overwhelmed with anxiety and rather than be filled with hope, we are consumed with despair. The enemy knows that the only way to stop you and I from being all we have been created to be in Christ and to live a life of joy and fulfilment, is to strip us of the belief that you and I are great, and can be made whole in Christ. However, if we counteract those negative thoughts and feelings with the positive action of faith, we are able to make a comeback from whatever depths we might find ourselves. Faith is an enabler to those who have chosen to live their lives by faith. In the midst of a dark season of life, faith switches on the light, even if it's a faint light that enables you and I to see our way out of every situation.

When I was younger, I got myself involved in more fights than I can remember. Irrespective of the size of the opposition, their reputation or past glories, I had a strong conviction inside of me that I could intimidate the opposition with my bragging and stories of made up victories. I realised that after a while, the person who I was intending to scuffle with would now start acting like a pigeon caught in a room full of cats. As I grew in confidence due to my own hype, I could see that the opposition was there for the taking. I would then move to quickly start slapping the opposition around, and then bask in the cheers and praise of my ASBO association peers. This is exactly how faith works!

Irrespective of what opposes us, irrespective of the size or strength of the opposition, we are to tell the opposition about our faith, brag about our faith in Christ, boast about how awesome our God is until the enemy starts to grow weary and we become stronger. In every situation of life, we are to live a life of faith to quench every fear and revoke all negativity. Those who choose to live by faith and utilise their faith as a weapon, have a strong conviction on the inside that the battle is not over until they win...

As we walk through the highways and street corners of life, I implore you to walk with your faith on a leash, letting the world know that you cannot be intimidated by circumstances, illness, job loss, rejection, broken promises, a broken heart, or financial collapse. The enemy will roar at you, but fight back with faith. Faith can counteract every negative report, every dark moment and every second of uncertainty in life.

In times of temptation, faith reminds us of who we truly are in Christ, and the assured promise that awaits those who remain faithful. Therefore, against temptation and wrongful desires, faith can be utilised as the weapon of choice to say 'NO!' to whatever presents itself as desirable. Many of us feel helpless and defeated whenever we find ourselves in compromising situations, in scenarios where we are being tempted, whether morally, sexually or ethically. Having a strong basis of faith allows us to gather the required will power and strength to rise above the temptation, to flee the scene and get back on track on the road to our destiny. Faith utilised in times of temptation and moral weakness enables us to keep our eyes on the bigger picture, and fight the good fight of faith! (Pun intended)

In short, my faith is my weapon, what's yours?

Great ideas about faith...

"There is nothing that wastes the body like worry, and one who has any faith in God should be ashamed to worry about anything whatsoever" – MAHATMA GANDHI

" Faith is to believe what you do not see; the reward of this faith is to see what you believe." – ANONYMOUS

"When you have come to the edge of all light that you know, and are about to drop off into the darkness of the unknown. Faith is knowing one of two things will happen: There will be something solid to stand on or you will be taught to fly" - PATRICK OVERTON

"Faith is deliberate confidence in the character of God whose ways you may not understand at the time." - OSWALD CHAMBERS

My Thoughts

3

Faith Works

"Wasn't our ancestor Abraham "made right with God by works" when he placed his son Isaac on the sacrificial altar? Isn't it obvious that faith and works are yoked partners, that faith expresses itself in works? That the works are "works of faith?" The full meaning of "believe" in the Scripture sentence, "Abraham believed God and was set right with God," includes his action. It's that mesh of believing and acting that got Abraham named "God's friend." Is it not evident that a person is made right with God not by a barren faith but by faith fruitful in works?" – James 2: 21-24, (The Message Bible)

I have come across many people in my lifetime who have spoken, preached, taught and testified about the greatness of their faith. However, when push came to shove, when they were struck by an unexpected life changing circumstance, their 'great faith' went AWOL. The amazing, yet underemphasised thing about faith is that real faith works!

Indeed and rightly so, we are saved and justified by faith in Christ Jesus; however our works, or simply put, the workings of our faith is what justifies and proves the genuineness of the very faith that we profess about.

In the Bible, when James talks about 'faith without works is dead...', he is rightfully saying that when we say we have faith, it causes us to 'work', it causes us to act! Real faith calls us to action. Real faith cannot be degraded to merely feelings, positive thinking, optimistic conscious decisions or passive mental processing. Faith in its true essence is a response. Whenever we respond to something, someone or a circumstance we are carrying out an action.

Even in our salvation, works is very much involved. Faith involves three crucial aspects or steps: knowledge, agreement and trust. Firstly we must have knowledge of the Saviour and His redemptive powers; secondly we must agree that we are in need of a Saviour; thirdly, we must approach Him, trusting that only He can save us. It is not the works that we do that saves us; however once we are saved by grace through our faith in Christ, it causes us to work.

Oftentimes we refer to incidents whereby we are called to do something 'unknown', take a risk, enter a new relationship after a difficult breakup etc, as taking a 'leap of faith.' The very connotation signifies that in order to truly have faith, or display faith, we must 'put our faith where our mouth is.

Faith that works is the only visible evidence that others can see that shows that we are truly people of faith. The Bible teaches us that '...by their fruits you shall know them...' In essence, we can only tell if someone has great faith by how they 'work their faith' or demonstrate their faith. Yes, we are justified by faith, but faith is justified (proven) by our works. A faith that works leads us to repentance, it leads us to obedience, it leads us to making morally and ethically right decisions even when no one is watching. Real faith that works leads us to living for an audience of one, it leads to having a servant heart, it leads to giving, it leads to us not taking shortcuts, it leads to checking our character constantly.

Although God can truly read our hearts, our thoughts and our minds; others cannot. Therefore it is by 'working our faith', not just in words but by our actions, that others can truly see we are people of faith.

Mike Murdoch once coined the phrase; 'Pursuit is the evidence of desire.' This is true for every area of our lives, but most importantly our faith. To pursue something, is to be actively going after, or working towards, a goal or desired destination. Therefore our faith (desire) must be coupled with a determined pursuit (works) that other people can view, and conclude that not only do we talk faith, but we live a lifestyle that demonstrates our faith.

In my earlier years of ministry, I was asked to pray for a young man who had been diagnosed with a life threatening disease, and was at that time severely ill in a hospital bed. I had great faith that God could heal him, however, one of my mentors challenged me to 'take a leap of faith' and visit the hospital and reject the prognosis or death sentence issued by the doctors. I must admit, I became weary and almost discouraged by the possibility of looking like a fool by walking into a large central London hospital and telling the doctors that I disagree with their professional diagnosis regarding the young man, not based on my years of medical practice, nor on my extensive research into the disease, but on my faith in Christ!... This is when I realised that we can easily say we have faith, but we only truly prove that faith by using it as an active response to a situation. After twice visiting the hospital, praying for the young man and cheekily letting the doctors know; they were wrong, a phone call came from a relative of the young man to inform me that the disease was receding, and that he was responding to medication, meaning that he was no longer deemed as 'terminally ill... 9 years on, he's still strong and loving the Lord. This is an example of me (admittedly reluctantly at first), working my faith.

I want to encourage and urge you to demonstrate your faith in every scenario of life. Whatever hand life deals you, utilise every ounce of faith you have to go through it, fight back, press on and never quit. As people of faith, we know deep down within us that the game is never over until we win. When the enemy attacks you, disturbs your peace, or comes in to torment you; know that it is time to activate and flaunt your faith. Faith whispers to us that 'victory is assured.' Faith knows how the story ends, and tells us that at the end of the film, '...all things work out together for our good!...'

Real faith itself is a great enabler. Real faith enables us to pursue God-sized dreams, manifest great visions, journey to uncharted territories, run faster, dig deeper and see the oasis in the midst of life's desert places.

Now put your faith to work...

Great ideas about faith...

"You block your dream when you allow your fear to grow bigger than your faith." – MARY MANIN MORRISSEY

"Faith isn't faith until it's all you're holding on to" - ANONYMOUS

"Fear can keep us up all night long, but faith makes one fine pillow." – PHILIP GULLEY

"Faith is like electricity. You can't see it, but you can see the light." – ANONYMOUS

My Thoughts

4

Growing Faith

'So then faith comes by hearing, and hearing from the Word of God' – Romans 10:17 (NKJV)

Naturally, many of us have a deep desire to grow, a desire to be better, a desire to mature as a person, and in every facet of our lives. Inversely, many of us also have a desire to take our faith to the next level. Growth is a natural aspect of human life. In fact, every living thing must grow. When growth ceases, then we can easily conclude that death has occurred.

We must make every effort to 'grow up' in our faith and strengthen our walk of faith. There is no magic wand or microwavable 'instant faith builder' that will cause you or me to become someone of great faith. Just like a plant grows in the soil and matures until it eventually bears fruit, our growing faith must also come through a process. This process can last a life time to reach maturity.

A plant needs water, soil and sun in order to grow. Physiologically, we all need nourishment in order to grow, body builders need to pump iron in order to strengthen and grow their muscles. Growing in faith is not dissimilar. For you and I to grow in faith we must be committed to getting the right nourishment that will feed our faith, we need to be exposed to the right conditions and environment that will enable us to grow, and we must exercise the faith we already have in order to take our faith to the desired next level.

Romans 10:17 highlights to us that faith comes by hearing. Not just simply hearing but hearing from the Word of God. What we hear is as important as who we are hearing it from. To say that 'faith comes' denotes that faith needs to arrive from a source, and that whatever is spoken needs to be received. The Word of God is food for spiritual growth. It is this food that causes and enables us to grow in faith and to understand what God is saying about situations or seasons we are experiencing.

Many of us become disheartened whenever we are unable to understand or 'see' what God is doing, or where He is taking us whenever we go through trials, tests and storms. However, those who are able to stand firm, and keep believing God even in the midst of adversities and uncertainties, are those who are able to understand and hold unto what God has spoken to them. Simply put, the more we are exposed to God's Words, the more we learn about Him and how He operates. We then learn about His principles, which in turn increases our confidence in Him, which inversely grows our faith.

Through spending time with God, we become educated, enlightened, encouraged, empowered and we are able to endure, because our faith has been enriched through feeding. The Word of God is the starting point for anyone who desires to grow in faith.

To continue to grow in faith, there are various ways this can happen:

Faith is grown through adversity...

People not only grow in favourable conditions, but oftentimes we are forced to grow because of the extremity of our environment and adverse situations. Many of us have heard of 'growing pains'. With every level of growth comes the price of the pain that is associated with it. Because of the associated pain, many people choose to remain in their comfort zone, and shy from any form of growth. Most athletes, and people dedicated to losing weight know very well that without pain, success is merely an illusion. The phrase 'no pain, no gain', is relevant to our faith growth. In the scriptures, Peter talks about 'trials of faith', because what is true is that at times our faith is forced to grow through a trial, a test or an adverse experience we go through.

Scripture also teaches us that we must endure trials, tribulations and troubles with patience, and that our faith must remain sure and strong. One of my favourite stories is about the three Hebrew boys in the book of Daniel, who were thrown into a hot burning furnace. The heat was so extreme that it killed the guards who threw them into the furnace. But, what was amazing was what they told king Nebuchadnezzar just before they were thrown into the furnace.

Shadrach, Meshach, and Abednego, answered and said to the king, "O Nebuchadnezzar, we are not careful to answer thee in this matter. If it be so, our God whom we serve is able to deliver us from the burning fiery furnace, and he will deliver us out of thine hand, O king. But if not, be it known unto thee, O king, that we will not serve thy gods, nor worship the golden image which thou hast set up." -Daniel 3:16-18 (KJV)

The incredible thing is that these three amazing young men knew they were in the hands of THE KING and not a king. They knew Who had the REAL power. Despite the adversity, their faith grew. In summary, their faith went something like this: "We belong to God. We are His boys. He has the ability to save us. He knows about our troubles. He hears our prayers. He is a faithful God. Whatever God decides to do with us, is because it is His will. We are therefore happy to surrender to the will of God in this and every situation." Often times God will allow us to go through adversity in order to grow us up in our faith in Him.

Faith is grown through experience...

In life, experience usually leads to confidence. We have more confidence in a GP who has many years of experience in his or her field, than a junior doctor straight out of medical school. Many of us also display more confidence in an area of life that we have more experience in, because we believe in our abilities. This is also true in terms of growing our faith.

Our faith also grows through our experience of seeing or witnessing God come through for us or others in the past. The Word exposes us to ancient stories of people who God came through for, and how that same Biblical story can be our story. Many of us can recall a time when God has turned up and helped us or delivered us from a very tight spot. That past experience of God's faithfulness encourages and energises us to keep believing that the God who did it then, can most definitely do it again.

To myself and millions of people around the world, Michael Jordan is regarded as the greatest basketball player that has ever lived. He is well known for making game winning shots and winning numerous NBA championships. Because of his experience and execution of making incredible, jaw-dropping shots, his coach and team mates during his playing days as a Chicago Bulls guard, would always run plays to get MJ open for him to take the last shot in a close game. Why? Because experience told them that, if they got the ball into his hands, more times than none, he would win the game with the last shot.

Oftentimes, experiencing God's ability to bring us through, enables us to grow in our confidence and faith in Him.

In Scripture, when the young boy David was facing up to Goliath, his confidence was boosted because of his own personal experience of seeing God in action. He taunted Goliath confidently by saying that the same God who delivered the lion and the bear into his hands, will also ensure that Goliath too, will become a fallen giant (pun fully intended!)

Experience is indeed a great teacher and also a key ingredient in the water we need to grow and flourish in faith.

Faith grows through prayer...

'If you don't ask, you don't get'... a simple and well known statement, yet we shy away from it when it comes to matters of faith. Many of us have never asked God for more faith.

In life, we all go through times that we struggle in our faith, yet we are able to actually request for a greater measure of faith from God. The Word tells us that we should ask, seek and knock... and we shall receive, find and experience open doors. Therefore, whenever we are in a situation that demands more faith, or requires a greater measure of faith to counteract the negativity we are experiencing, we can simply pray and ask God to fill us up.

We must learn in times of weakness to ask for God's assistance, as His strength is perfected when we are experiencing weakness, discouragement or weariness.

So go on, soak yourself in the Word, draw on experience, see the good in adversity, pray without ceasing, and in turn, grow in faith.

Great ideas about faith...

"Without faith a man can do nothing; with it all things are possible." - SIR WILLIAM OSLER

"All I have seen teaches me to trust the Creator for all I have not seen." - RALPH WALDO EMERSON

"Faith is deliberate confidence in the character of God whose ways you may not understand at the time." OSWALD CHAMBERS

My Thoughts

5

Faith That Sticks

'It was by faith that Moses left Egypt and was not afraid of the king's anger. Moses continued strong as if he could see the God that no one can see.' – Hebrews 11:27 (NCV)

The key to success in our faith-walk and our Christian living is the same as it was for Christ and all the faithful heroes we study about in the Bible. True spiritual success is found in our ability to endure. As people of faith we should never be quitters. Throughout the bible, we are encouraged over and over again to endure, to stick with it, to stay in the fight till the very end.

One of the easiest things to do in life is to start! We find it easy to start a course, start a job, start reading a book, start a relationship, start a weight loss regime, start believing, start a new journey; on the flip side, one of the hardest things to do is to see it through to the very end. Endurance is one of those things that comes through being able to see the finish line, the bigger picture and being a person of discipline. For example, believe it or not, I have a desire to not be this skinny preacher boy for the rest of my life, so, what did I do? I started a weight gain and exercise program, notice that I said started, those who have seen me recently may have noticed that I am yet to endure.....you need faith that endures, otherwise, you will remain in the same state- skinny like me.

In life there are some things that we should quit; quit smoking, quit playing games with God, quit telling those dirty jokes in order to fit into the crowd. However, we should understand that when it comes to waiting on God, and trusting God, we should never quit!

We need to stick to what we believe, irrespective of the contrary tangible evidences.

I can attest to the notion that our faith is always in a test. For most of us we feel like all hell is breaking loose all around us, everything we have come to know is falling apart. These are the times we know that our faith is being tested. In circumstances like these, the easiest thing to do is to quit and give up, to stop trying, stop believing and stop pursuing. But we must realise that great faith is interwoven with great trials, and must always go through great tests in order to prove its authenticity.

I have great admiration for marathon runners. I previously lived in an area of London that formed part of the route for the annual London Marathon. I had a vantage point, which allowed me to see marathon runners of all shapes, sizes and abilities pant very heavily as they ran the 26.3 miles of the marathon. The intriguing thing about the marathon is that, not everyone who started the race, finished it. Each year thousands of people set off at the start of the marathon, with a genuine belief and desire that they will make it to the finish line, especially as they have taken their bodies and lungs through relentless preparation. However, a time comes along the marathon route, when fatigue and cramps creeps in and inversely some of the runners will drop out. Those who's desire and determination outweighs their fatigue are able to 'press on' towards their goal of the finish line irrespective of their aches and pains. Those who finish have engraved in them the notion of 'no victory without conflict.'

Real faith teaches us that in order to have great victory, we must endure great conflicts. Conflict and tests are the backdrops on which victory shines the best. As people of faith, we need to understand that without rain there is no rainbow, without war there are no spoils. Therefore, we need a faith that sticks through the storms, trials, valleys, troubles and uncertainties of life, because we are pressing on towards what lies on the other side of our tests.

The book of James Chapter 1:12 tells us that...'God blesses those who patiently endure testing and temptation. Afterward they will receive the crown of life that God has promised to those who love him.' (Paraphrased)

The ability to endure, to be tenacious and relentless is a vital part of walking with God and walking by faith. Faith has the ability to propel us to great heights, however we need to also be also to stick around in times of great lows.

Waiting on God and sticking with Him is often a great challenge, and goes against everything that our natural sensory organs pick up from our 'quick fix', microwave, 'just add water' culture, where we want everything in an instant. We want our healing now, our blessings now, our husbands now, our debts wiped out now. But I believe that we need to understand that faith is not just a component to drop things on our lap, and make things miraculously happen. Faith also has a mandate to cause us to grow. Oftentimes, it is in the process of waiting, just as we would wait for a plant to grow and blossom, that we are transformed, challenged, strengthened and changed.

We always pray for 'faith that will move mountains', but in addition, we should also pray for faith that will not cause us to be moved or shaken. Many believers forfeit their breakthrough, because of their inability to stick around and therefore negate the need to sometimes wait. We need to build a faith that will endure, that will stick around long enough to receive from God.

In Christian circles, a powerful phrase is often thrown around: 'Can you stand to be blessed?' I truly believe that the question this phrase posses carries more weight than we usually attach to it. 'Can you stand to blessed?', can be interpreted as, are you willing and able despite how long it takes, and how bad it looks, to stick around, wait on God to receive from Him?'

The testing of real faith produces patience, and it is that patience that enables us to finish well, witness vision come to life and accomplish greatness.

Faith is saying to you, "how bad do you want it?"
'For you know that when your faith is tested, your endurance has a chance to grow'. James 1:3 (NLT)

When we come to the realisation that God is our one and only option, we will stick with Him and rely on His promises. Our faith needs to get to a place whereby we can always see the bigger picture, where we can see beyond the now, where we can see that even if our circumstances are not feasibly changing, we can see that God is changing us, and we can see through our faith, the finish line.

Get your glue out; you need faith that sticks!

Great ideas about faith...

'Don't give up. Don't ever give up.'
– JIMMY VALVANO, LEGENDARY BASKETBALL COACH

'Real faith is enduring faith. Fake faith withers in tough times.'
– RICK WARREN via Twitter

'Faith isn't faith until it's all you're holding on to.' – ANONYMOUS

'A faith that hasn't been tested can't be trusted.'
– ADRIAN ROGERS

My Thoughts

6

Hope... Faith's Foundation

'Now faith is the substance of things hoped for, the evidence of things not seen. For by it the elders obtained a good testimony.'
– Hebrews 11:1 – 2 (NKJV)

According to God's Word, Faith is the substance of things we hope for. Therefore, without hope, faith has no substance. Hope can be intertwined with the word: Expectation. To have hope is to have expectation of an outcome, and our faith is what substantiates that expectation by driving us towards what we expect. We ride on the train of faith, because we expect to arrive at a destination.

We've often heard of the saying that 'there are never any hopeless situations, just people who have stopped hoping'. One of the greatest tragedies of life is when a person or a community of people, whether it be a family, a church, a nation, a sports team etc stop expecting, and stop hoping. The heartbeat of every human being, Christian or not, is our innate expectation for something, or a situation to change. In winter, we look on with great anticipation and expectation of sun bathing in the summer months, we expect new relationships and friendships to be better than our ex's, we expect that when we buy a new pair of jeans from Ted Baker, that we are buying something of quality. In essence, we exercise our faith, because we have a hope.

When building a house, we are often told that the foundation we build upon is as important as what we build. Therefore, as people of faith, what we are hoping for needs to be something made of strong stuff.

In recent times, many of us witnessed the story of the thirty three Chilean Miners, who were trapped underground in a collapsed coal mine for sixty nine days, and came out triumphant in what has been classed as a miracle. Their story is one of a near death experience, and hope. After being trapped, these men were able to give each other hope in the face of what appeared to be certain death, and overcame the fear that confronted them. Their emotional and Hollywood ending story is also one of how the human spirit can still hope in the midst of what many would have seen as a hopeless situation. They were triumphant over fear, depression, and a horror that many of us could not imagine.

We often feel inferior or undeserving of applying the same faith, expressed by the miners in our own circumstances. We've almost become by default, couch-potato miracle spectators. Settled to just watching others experience miracles and breakthroughs, rather than expecting to experience our own miracles firsthand. The miners were thirty three ordinary men who found themselves in a crazy situation. All they had was hope. Hope to see their families again, hope that they would be able to hug their loved ones, possibly hope that they would be able to cheer on their favourite football teams again, hope that they would be able to enjoy their favourite homemade dishes again. It was their hope, their expectation, that pulled them through. One of the miners, after being rescued, said in an interview for Chilean TV, that whilst trapped in the coal mine, he believed that Jesus Christ still had work for him to do, and that he was expecting to do that work. That was what kept him going.

At some points in our lives, many of us feel like our entire world is caving in and collapsing around us, we feel trapped and hopeless.

However, I have come to realise that as long as we have an expectation of how things ought to be, or turn out; if we can conjure up enough faith to sustain our hope, we are on our road to victory.

Even in the midst of death, we have an assured hope and expectation that our loved ones will wake up once again on the day of resurrection. Our faith through Christ's own resurrection, and His promises to us, strengthens our faith as we anticipate with eagerness that glorious day.

What appears to be hopeless situations are merely incidents when we need our faith to be refilled in order to enable us to see how the story plays out. Even if all we get is a little crack in the dark cave we find ourselves in that is sufficient. The Chilean Miners' faith was fuelled and refilled the moment when they heard the first faint voice shouting down from above ground.

In the States, a man approached a little league baseball game one afternoon. He asked a boy in the dugout what the score was. The boy responded, "Eighteen to nothing--we're behind." "Boy," said the spectator, "I'll bet you're discouraged." "Why should I be discouraged?" replied the little boy. "We haven't even gotten up to bat yet!" This young boy knew in his heart that his team were still in the game, and they should not be counted out just because of how scary the oppositions lead was. Whenever, we are able to hold unto hope, irrespective of how faint that hope might be, we kick discouragement out of the equation, and can anticipate a good ending.

Every morning we should spring out of our bed with great expectation for the day ahead. Each new day is a gift from God, whether you're jobless, been given a negative medical diagnosis, going through a messy divorce, homeless, abandoned by your family and friends, you should see that with each new day, you have a brand new canvass to paint a master piece upon, you can anticipate and expect great things, through a great God, Who has great love for you.

Hopelessness is nothing more than an emotional state based on a perceived current situation. Hope is faith's reality and faith's ideal destination. However much our circumstances reminds us of the fact that life is not a bed of roses; hope makes one fine pillow to rest our head upon as we anticipate better!

Hoping is free, you should get some...

Great ideas about faith...

'Without faith, nothing is possible. With it, nothing is impossible.'
- MARY MCLEOD BETHUNE

'Faith is putting all your eggs in God's basket, then counting your blessings before they hatch.' - RAMONA C. CARROLL

'Where hope grows, miracles blossom.' - ELNA RAE

"Let your hopes, not your hurts, shape your future."
- ROBERT H SCHULLER

My Thoughts

7

Crazy Faith

"But without faith it is impossible to please Him: for he who comes to God must believe that He is, and that He is a rewarder of them that diligently seek Him." – Hebrews 11:6 (NKJV)

Once in a while, we are all confronted with situations that requires for us to act like we are on crazy pills. We have all encountered people in our lives, who we secretly (or publically) believe are a little 'cuckoo ', people we classify as having a few cookies short of a full cookie jar, people who tend to act, talk crazy and see things that are not really there. However, if we look closely enough at what faith really is, don't we all have to have a crazy streak about us in order to really live by faith? Being crazy isn't always a bad thing, if we are crazy enough to believe that God is all that we need.

Faith is an unwavering, unquestioning and unfailing belief, reliance and trust in God irrespective of what you can or cannot see. We are prompted through God's Words that our faith must be certain, unmoving and hopeful in God. In essence we are putting complete trust and reliance unto God; Someone we cannot see, about an answer we are yet to receive, and about something we have no physical evidence of it's existence. Doctors would call this behaviour irrational whilst psychiatrists might classify this as insanity and would seek to section a person who displays these characteristics into a mental institution.

Unfortunately, we live in a world where we are more dependant and reliant on the things we see, rather than exercising our faith, in order for us not be classified as crazy. Even some so called Christians' shy away from truly living by faith in order to fit into the crowd, as opposed to being disfranchised from normality, and political correctness. Paul reminds us in Hebrews 11:6, that without faith, it is impossible to please God. Some people are more concerned about pleasing people, and fitting in, rather than exercising some crazy faith. In order to please God, we need to fully live by faith, even in crazy situations. The crazier and more intense the situation appears, the more crazy faith we need to put into practice.

In our journey of life, we will all come across crazy situations, which are so pressing and intense that it has the propensity to drive us crazy. In situations that do not make sense, we don't understand how we are supposed to get out of this tight place. Crazy situations such as being diagnosed with a terminal illness, losing financial stability, losing a loved one unexpectedly, can leave people, on the verge of an emotional, physical and mental breakdown. However, when we are able to laugh in the face of adversity, and look at our crazy situations, and say 'my faith is crazier than my crazy situation', then we are able to experience some crazy results.

In the Bible, Daniel and the three Hebrew boys who were on the verge of being sacrificed because they refused to defile themselves, were truly exercising some crazy faith. Rather than taking part in the king's feast, and being part of the king's entourage, they chose beyond what seemed logical and preferred to go unto death in order to show that their God was able to rescue them even in the midst of a fiery furnace. What was even crazier was the fact that they were prepared to place their lives in the hands of God even if God did not deliver them.

Those around them must have thought these young boys had totally lost their minds. However, the boys knew with total conviction and with unwavering belief that; when the going gets tough, their faith must get tougher and crazier.

Recently, I came across a young man who had graduated from university over 4 years ago, but could not obtain employment in his field. One day after a period of praying and fasting, he decided to give it one final push. He applied for a role within one of the largest companies in his industry; however the position applied for required him to have had 5 years of checkable work experience in the role. Trusting God, the young man applied for the role without any exaggeration on his CV. (How many of us are bold enough to do that?) He went on to the West End to purchase the most expensive suit he could afford in preparation for an interview he was yet to be shortlisted for, which was dependant on a CV that was likely the weakest in the pool of applicants. The application deadline came and went without any response. A week later he called the company, and mentioned that he was awaiting confirmation of his interview date. The receptionist on the other line literally laughed at him, as she remarked that all successful applicants had already interviewed for the role and the Directors were on the verge of making an offer to one of the interviewees. Undeterred, the young man went on to request for his call to be put through to the Director's office, which the receptionist professionally declined. Once again undeterred, he found the Director's name on Twitter, and sent him a short message simply stating "I'm the guy you are looking for, I can bring great creativity and tenacity to your company. I don't have the experience, but I have faith in my abilities and some crazy ideas that will add value to the organisation". Another week went past, and no response. The young man sent another message 'I'm still expecting a response, I'm ready to start next week. All I need is 10 minutes to prove myself'

A few days later, something crazy happened. This young man received a phone call from the Director, saying how he loved the young man's tenacity, drive, and craziness in using a social networking site to reapply for a job he wasn't qualified for. To cut a very long story short, he started a week later, on a pay package that blew his mind away, and was given a 6 week intensive workshop to fast-track his experience.

About a month later, I met up at a Central London Starbucks with this young man, as we sat down over a cup of hot chocolate, with tears streaming down his cheeks, he said to me 'Hey PG, do you know that this whole experience has been one crazy ride?', I nodded in agreement. He went on to say 'Crazy things do happen to people with crazy faith. Even I thought I was crazy at first.'

As people of faith, we often have to go beyond caring what others think about us, in order to receive and experience what God has for us. Having crazy faith in a midst of a crazy situation doesn't mean that you are in insane, it just means that your faith in God is stronger and more rooted than how you see your situation. The world might laugh at you, call you names, ostracise you and say you are crazy. However you and I know that crazy times, require crazy measures of faith. It's not what people say about you or your situation that matters, it's what God says.

Are you crazy enough to trust God?

Great ideas about faith...

“Seeds of faith are always within us; sometimes it takes a crisis to nourish and encourage their growth.” - SUSAN TAYLOR

“We are twice armed if we fight with faith.” – PLATO

“The only limit to our realization of tomorrow will be our doubts of today. Let us move forward with strong and active Faith.”
– THEODORE ROOSEVELT

“Weave in faith and God will find the thread.” – A PROVERB

My Thoughts

8

'Yes' Faith

"It was by faith that Abraham obeyed when God called him to leave home and go to another land that God would give him as his inheritance. He went without knowing where he was going."
– Hebrews 11:8 (NLT)

As we journey through life, it's always encouraging and uplifting to have a mentor, a guide or a role model to help you know what's possible. I believe that faith is all about possibilities and expectations even in the midst of uncertainties, and when the road ahead looks unclear and cloudy. In the Bible, God points us towards Abraham as a 'Faith Mentor.'

Abraham is depicted in Scriptures as a person not only of faith, but obedient faith. Abraham was like anyone of us, a simple human being with faults and all. He had some good days, he had some bad days, he told a few lies here and there and he got scared every once in a while just like you and me; however, despite his human flaws, he was obedient. Abraham trusted God, and was unwavering in his obedience to whatever God required of him.

To put things into perspective, it's important to know exactly who Abraham was. Abraham was no spring chicken when God called him to leave his homeland. At age 75, he was to leave everything behind, and go on a journey, with no knowledge of his final destination. Most of us would find it rather difficult to just 'get up and go', especially if the person instructing us to go, withholds from us where exactly we are to go. In order to truly be a person of faith, we must have an unwavering and unshakeable trust and confidence in God irrespective of the information presented or lack of information at hand.

Obedient faith comes from saying 'yes' despite you not having the full information of how the story will play out. Many of us work on logic, some of us are calculated and we 'count the cost' and weigh up the risks and rewards, before agreeing to any requests or invitation. On the flip side, obedient faith doesn't require to see how the story plays out, it doesn't require any hard facts or evidence, neither does it require a well drawn out map. Obedient faith agrees and trusts, not dependent on the request being made, but rather on the person making the request.

As a person growing in faith, we must be able to take God at His word, and follow Him wherever he calls us to go. I truly believe that, rather than waiting to receive the full information or itinerary of where God is calling you or me to, we need to trust that He Who has called us, will also work out the fine details.

In the summer of 2005, I felt God calling me to embark on a major Kingdom assignment. However, I didn't have the full information, the resources, nor did I have a clue of how I was going to accomplish such a huge task. I still agreed to go along on the ride, destination – unknown. Not only did I not have the full information of how things would turn out, I also didn't have my own finances to pump into this project. However, through obedience, I realised that, along the way, God began to connect me with like-minded people who would be of great resource and encouragement. Funding was granted, above and beyond what was requested.

Abraham experienced great favour, and open doors, as soon as he obeyed God. Obedience precedes favour. Whenever we make a choice to obey God, despite not knowing the fine details, God now has room to manoeuvre and use you and I to do amazing things that will leave us, and others who witness our obedience with dropped jaws in amazement.

The Bible reminds us that ' without faith, it is impossible to please God'; therefore, our obedient faith is something that truly pleases and delights God. God has a habit of pouring out blessings and favour upon those who please Him through their obedience and confidence in Him.

To test Abraham's faith at a whole-nother-level, God called out Abraham to sacrifice the son he had 'sweated' to have. All along, Abraham possessed an unshakable and unmistakable confidence that God was about to show Himself as a provider. As the story pans out, we recall that God provided an alternative sacrifice, just as Abraham believed.

Our level of faith is measured by the level of our obedience. As we walk in obedience, we are not merely following orders, but rather, we are following the One Who is making the requests, or giving the instructions.

A family friend was given a huge task, to organise a retreat for young people to go out into the English countryside to spend a weekend. More than forty people expressed their interest in going on the retreat. However, when it came time to make payments, many people were unable to do so, but were still interested in attending the weekend away. This young lady had to make a choice to either fork out the full payment amount for forty or so people, or cancel the retreat, even though she knew it was a God inspired vision, and the fact that many lives would be blessed through the time away from the hustle and bustle of our capital city. She decided on the former, using funds intended for a deposit on her first property to pay for everyone to attend the retreat.

A few months later, she spoke to me and mentioned how God had compensated and rewarded her obedience. She received a cheque from a secret donor who just wanted to bless her ministry. The cheque amount was more than she had sacrificed in paying for everyone to attend what was a truly amazing retreat.

Many of us have been given a God-sized vision or instruction, yet our response should never be one of doubt or questioning, it should be one of 'yes'. True faith is obeying God, and allowing Him to work out the fine details whenever, you are called to move by faith "All you gotta do is say yes!"

Great ideas about faith...

"We are twice armed if we fight with faith." - PLATO

"The way to see by faith is to shut the Eye of Reason."
– BENJAMIN FRANKLIN

'The smallest seed of faith is better than the largest fruit of happiness.'
- HENRY DAVID THOREAU

'To me faith means not worrying.' - JOHN DEWEY

My Thoughts

9

Faith Expects...

'But those who hope in the LORD will renew their strength; They will soar on wings like eagles; they will run and not grow weary, they will walk and not be faint.' - Isaiah 40:31 (NKJV)

Expectation is defined as 'the act or the state of expecting; an expectant mental attitude'. In its rawest form, faith is all about expectation! We expect because we have a committed trust in Whom we have expectation in.

Many of us have experienced the feeling of looking forward to something promised, something anticipated. I remember as a child, looking forward to my first ever trip to Chessington World of Adventures. I had heard the stories from other children, I had seen the exciting and mouth watering adverts on TV, and now I was merely a day away from experiencing this phenomena first hand. The excitement kept me up all through the night. I just couldn't sleep a wink. As I anticipated experiencing this amazing thrill, it did not matter what else was going on around me, or what other people were saying. At that point, it did not matter that I had had a challenging day at school, or the fact that I missed my favourite television shows. The excitement was just too much for me to be distracted or concerned about anything else. Although tired and jaded, when morning came, the excitement caused me to act as if I had drunk ten cans of RedBull- I had wings!

I'm certain you too can recall times in your life when your expectation of a thing, event, or a someone (we've all had a crush!) caused you to have butterflies in your belly, or to wear a grin on your face from ear to ear. The key fact is that true faith expects, and that expectation causes us to have renewed strength, and become blind to the negativities or the opposition around us. When we have a faith that is real, it has the propensity to give us a lift, it causes us to rise above those things in life which are fearful and discouraging, because we are looking around the corner waiting for our situation to change, believing that God is able to turn things around in our favour.

While we may not always get what we want, we will always get what we expect! Expectation has the power and propensity to breathe life into a dead situation, it has the power to cause you and I to go beyond every opposition, negative thought or imagination and create our own reality. A reality that is powered by faith. At the same time, expectation also has the power to bring to life all the negative things you perceive for your future, so base your expectation on positive things only.

When we expect, we are demonstrating a belief system that anticipates a favourable and positive eventuality or outcome. When we fail to have expectations, we are drowned in doubt, discouragement and feelings of failure and defeat. We expect because we believe deep down in our core that God is able to meet our expectations.

I have met people who go through life without expectations, or anticipating any positive eventuality in their lives. This is mainly due to a previous negative experience, or an ingrained negative affirmation, which has sapped every ounce of expectation and hopefulness out of them. Whenever I come in contact with these individuals, they are unable to get excited about anything or anyone.

Even good news is received with caution, as they ironically expect the ending to turn out bad.

People of faith make up in their mind that no matter the opposition, no matter their past negative experience, irrespective of the report; they will place their confidence totally in God, because they believe this time, He will come through. Unbelievers will call this delusion or foolishness, however we know that God has a good record of meeting and exceeding the expectations of those who love Him, who trust Him, and who wait on Him.

Weeping endures for a night, but joy comes in the morning... therefore, as you cry 'boo woo woo...' keep one eye open, and expect the floodgates of heaven to open up for you, by faith expect God to bring you out and bring you through...

Believers are people of great expectations, because believers are connected to an awesome, great and faithful God Who does great, amazing, jaw-dropping miracles! Our faith tells us, that we are next in line for a miracle!

Expect that God will deliver you and turn things around.

Great ideas about faith...

"Believe that when you come into the presence of God you can have all you came for. You can take it away, and you can use it, for all the power of God is at your disposal in response to your faith."
- SMITH WIGGLESWORTH

"Seeds of faith are always within us; sometimes it takes a crisis to nourish and encourage their growth." – SUSAN TAYLOR

"To one who has faith, no explanation is necessary. To one without faith, no explanation is possible." - ST. THOMAS AQUINAS

"You block your dream when you allow your fear to grow bigger than your faith." - MARY MANIN MORRISSEY

My Thoughts

10

Faith Lenses

'For we live by believing, not by seeing' – 2 Corinthians 5:7 (NLT)

How we perceive life, circumstances and situations can literally make or break us. Many people have survived great trauma and catastrophes merely because they chose to see the situation through the lenses of faith.

Many of us are accustomed with the saying 'There is purpose in every pain'. This reminds and strengthens us to see God in every situation, every storm, every setback, every rejection, and in every season of wilderness and in every battle even the ones that appear to have been lost.

When we see and walk by faith, we are able to be like David, and to 'walk through the valley of the shadow...', endure persecution, endure seasons of wilderness, knowing that God is with us. Seeing life through the lenses of faith simply means being able to utilise all of the faith you and I have studied, heard about, developed and experienced, to filter every one of life's experiences and situations. Two people can go through the same situation, but have a different experience of that situation. This is due to the way they choose to filter and inversely react to the situation. In Scriptures we are able to witness how various characters chose to filter their circumstances through the lens of faith. David conquered Goliath because of His trust in God, and His ability to filter the great giant through the lens of faith. The lens of faith made the giant appear a midget compared to God.

When we filter life through the lens of faith, we are able to see our circumstances as what they truly are - minor things! In turn the lens of faith allows God to be magnified in every situation we encounter. A lens of faith magnifies God and minimises the strength of our storms. It strengthens us to truly believe that 'Greater is He Who is in you, than he who is in the world'. (1 John 4:4) When we exercise true and unwavering faith, we are able to see correctly, having a 20/20 vision which, rather than causing us to complain to God about how big the mountains and obstacles in our lives are, makes us gloat to the mountain and the obstacle of how great our God is. Every morning before I switch on the news channels, read the daily papers or switch on the laptop, I ensure that I have meditated on God's Word through the Bible, spent time reading my daily devotional, have my morning board meeting with God (prayers), sung a song or two of worship, tell my family I love them, affirm and confess that 'my sins are forgiven, I'm the head not the tail, I'm created in Christ's image, and I serve a God Who has great thoughts towards me'. Then, and only then, do I now allow myself to be exposed to the information of this world, which is usually negative, terrifying, carnal, contrary to my faith, panic inducing, esteem destroying, temptation ridden and just plain crazy! However, because of the fact that I have given the first portion of my day to God, and I'm filled with Him, I can then filter every negativity and every news headline, every phone call, every crazy driver on the road, every rejection, every obscenity, every business deal that falls through, even the little things that can mess up your day, like burnt toast, through the lens of faith.

When we filter things through the lens of faith, rather than panicking, losing our peace and saying 'Oh my God, what is going on here?', we are simply able to say 'Lord, what are you trying to say, teach me or reveal to me through this matter?'

Visions and dreams, in their simplest forms, are simply our ability as humans and believers to see more than and beyond what we see at present. It is the resolve to see what cannot be seen, and to use a filter that makes what appears humanly impossible, possible.

In life, our possibilities are proportionate to our faith. Whatever we can see and believe is possible, can happen. Too many people have given up on life, and on their dreams because they magnified the opposition and the risk of failure more than the possibilities.

I know of a property developer who has made a fortune out of buying derelict buildings at auction, in some of the UK's most undesirable areas, and turning them into luxurious homes, homes that would resemble something out of MTV Cribs. Many other would-be-developers passed on those same buildings because they were simply unable to see beyond the derelict and the ruins.

As people of faith, we must be able to look at the situations, pains, and challenges in our lives through the lens of faith, believing that God is involved in every circumstance and detail of our lives. We are not called to believe everything we see, but we are to see everything we believe. Therefore, ensure that you have the right filter that will enable you to see the roses amongst the thorns of life, rather than merely the thorns in your life.

What lens are you looking through?

Great ideas about faith...

'Faith is to believe what you do not yet see; the reward for this faith is to see what you believe' – ST AUGUSTIN

'There is no such thing as blind faith! Faith is not blind, rather it is the ability & the resolve to look through the lenses of possibilities' - G AJEWOLE

'The question is not what you look at, but what you see"
– HENRY DAVID THOREAU

'...Put on your spiritual glasses, in time uncertainty passes. If you would only trust Him completely...'
– SELONE AJEWOLE, SONGWRITER
(lyrics from the song; 'Human Eyes')

My Thoughts

11

Faithllionaire

'And my God will meet all your needs according to his glorious riches in Christ Jesus.' – Philippians 4:19 (NIV)

Recently, I came across a very interesting article of a young man in the States, who became a self-made millionaire by the age of 14. In his best selling book entitled 'Reallionaire', Farrah Gray, the young African American explores the meaning of true wealth, and talks about his journey from humble beginnings to becoming a millionaire. In promoting his book, he went on The Mo'Nique show on BET, and explained the title for his book. In his dissection of the title 'Reallionaire', Farrah explains that many people in the world have material riches, yet they are living a miserable life, whilst he knew of people without financial security who are happier than those with riches.

After studying this young man's story and taking an interest in his perception of true wealth, I was prompted to coin up the phrase 'Faithllionaire', which speaks of being rich in faith. I believe that with faith we can create our own reality, choose how we respond to life's challenges and utilise that faith to call into existence all that we desire. I strongly believe that those who possess real faith are the true wealthy people on this earth- we have heard of the saying 'money cannot buy you happiness'.

Following the recent global economic meltdown, many people whose faith and confidence was in their jobs and finances were dealt a huge blow. Everything they had built up, had now literally disappeared right before their eyes. This has shown us that money comes, and money goes, jobs come and jobs go, friends come and go. So, there can be only one sure thing in this life, that's God! When we put our confidence in God, we are immune from the topsy-turvy nature of the world's economic climate, unemployment statistics, political uncertainties, threats of job losses, increased university fees, and sweet mouthed politicians.

I have come to realise that real wealth comes from knowing who you are, Whose you are, and understanding the level of greatness that lies inside each and everyone of us roaming this earth. To be rich in faith means to be confidently assured of the outcome, to be confident that 'the cattle on a thousand hills belong to God!' – Psalm 50:10 (paraphrased for emphasis). When we know that God owns everything, that He has the ability to give us all our needs and that He has the power to open and close doors, which money cannot buy, we are truly rich, abundantly rich.

I believe that people of faith, are the richest people in life. People who operate and approach every area of life, including their finances by faith understand the true concept of sowing and reaping. People of faith tithe, they give more to others, they understand the purpose of money, they know that God is the source of all wealth, they understand by faith that if they seek first the Kingdom, everything else will be added unto them. People of faith also understand that they are managers of money, and not slaves to it, they also understand that they are not merely consumers of goods, but rather they are to use their finances to glorify and worship God.

During our honeymoon in the Caribbean, my wife and I took a day out to leave behind the luxurious beach front hotels, and visited a remote village near the town of Higuey in the eastern region of the Dominican Republic. These are the images that never make the glossy holiday brochures that only show the paradise-esqe, 5 star, blue water side of this region of the world. In this village, we were confronted with people, young and old living in what I would classify as poverty. They would be classified as living in poverty, because they did not have the HD ready plasma TV, they didn't have a car, branded clothes, the latest trainers, Iphones, laptops, things that many have come to regard as some of life's necessities. However, they had such beautiful smiles, and were clearly happy with their lives. They might not have possessed all of the 'luxuries' we in the western world regard as essentials, but their standard of living, their life expectancy, their perception of life was something I was truly envious of. Many people are currently unhappy with their lives, merely because they covet what their neighbours have; we live in a culture where we are tempted through the media and society's infatuation with celebrities, to always strive to keep up with the Jones', by having the latest things. How can one ever be satisfied? How can we ever keep up? We are seeking God incorrectly to meet our wants and not our needs. The amazing souls that live in that village were content and happy, and had their faith recharged because, they understand that God is Santa Claus. They are happy because they know that God is meeting their needs, and if and when He chooses to meet their wants, that's a bonus. The level of faith displayed by the residents of the village, and in thousands of villages in Africa, Asia, Eastern Europe, the Pacific Islands, Latin America and even in some households in London, clearly shows that they have greater riches than the suit wearing types that fill out Wall Street and Canary Wharf.

True wealth is determined by our standard of life and our happiness. Our happiness is not derived by what or how much we have, but rather by knowing who we are, understanding Who we belong to, and the fact that everything belongs to Him.

When we have great faith, and great confidence in God – The Creator and Architect of all things, we are rich beyond our wildest dreams. I believe that God desires to bless each and everyone of us; however, we must keep our focus on the main thing – our walk with God, and a strong desire to please Him. God has the ability to change our financial situations, our employment status, without the need for us to compromise and take short cuts. You might finish reading this chapter, and still go to your bank account and see that you are in the red, your accountant might still tell you that you're on the brink of bankruptcy, but I still believe that if you place your hope in God, believe that He is 'able to do exceedingly, above all that you can fathom and conceive in your mind', and expect Him to, He can and He will turn things around for you. People of faith are rich, not because of what they have, but because of Who they have. That house, that job, that new car, that private school for the children, that church building fund, that missions trip to Asia, that new business venture, that new project, that young boy you want to sponsor through education in Ghana... it's all possible, because God has a funny, faith-induced way of exceeding our expectations and giving us the desires of our hearts, as long as we keep our minds stayed on Him.

In God's mind, if you live by faith and approach Him in faith, you are already more than a billionaire. Bill Gates, Oprah Winfrey, Carlos Slim, and Donald Trump have nothing on you! Forbes magazine might not have given you a call yet to appear on the front cover of their latest issue, no need to worry; you are on the front page of God's magazine, and He wants to show you off! I would rather be a Faithllionaire, spending in God's unlimited abundance, than the limited millions in the bank. Millionaires and Billionaires have their limits, but God has no limits! Not only is God our Provider, but He is also our provision.

Any Faithllionaires in the house?

Great ideas about faith...

'The blessings of The Lord, makes rich, and He adds no sorrow to it' – PROVERBS 10:22 (AMERICAN STANDARD BIBLE)

'Faith enables persons to be persons because it lets God be God.'
- CARTER LINDBERG

'A little faith will bring your soul to heaven, but a lot of faith will bring heaven to your soul.' - AUTHOR UNKNOWN

'Faith is taking the first step even when you don't see the whole staircase.' - MARTIN LUTHER KING JR

'Faith makes the discords of the present the harmonies of the future.'
- ROBERT COLLYER

My Thoughts

12

Separating Faith...

"If ye were of the world, the world would love his own; but because ye are not of the world, but I have chosen you out of the world, therefore the world hateth you." John 15:19 KJV

We all know that our environment and the company we keep can have either a positive or negative impact on our lives, our thinking and our sets of beliefs. Many people's faith, vision and dreams have been squashed by the atmosphere they are operating in, or by the people they allow to speak into their lives.

In our quest to pursue all that God has created you and I to be, we must separate ourselves from every negative influence and every voice that is contrary to the faith we uphold in Christ. Everyone of us needs a cheerleader or two in our lives, and the same goes for our walk of faith. If those around you, whether family, friends, colleagues or partners are constantly putting out the fire of your faith, by doubting your dreams and your victory, your breakthrough and your recovery, you must separate yourself from them. Separation is not merely a physical movement, but rather a re-alignment and a detachment from allowing negative words and negative influences to affect you.

In the Scriptures, we learn of how Noah was given a word from God that required him to build an ark to save his family and two of every kind of animal on earth from the impending floods. During this process, Noah had to separate himself from those around him, who were mocking him, and who were spreading rumors about him

Those who achieve greatness, and experience miracles, oftentimes have to be prepared to separate themselves from the status quo, and from the masses. True faith goes against the logic of rational, the norm and what is regarded as popular.

There comes a time in life when we have to make a decision with regard to whose voice we desire to listen to. We will have to choose between running with the crowd, staying in a state of mediocrity, or putting our full confidence in God. This is one of the most difficult things a believer can do, yet it is also a great expression of how much we trust in the power, authenticity and sovereignty of God. People of great faith have to be prepared to be ridiculed and mocked for a little while, without being deterred, neither relenting from their faith.

Walking by faith can sometimes lead to losing friendships, the comfort of a job, and family members. True faith does not allow us to fit into the crowd; on the contrary, it causes us to stand out from the crowd. True faith is outstanding, it's powerful, it's abnormal. The majority of people walking the face of this earth have settled for mediocrity, they have given up dreaming, they are only able to put their trust in things that they can feel, see and hear. Their ability to go higher has been diminished, they have accepted every report given to them, they have accepted their situation as irrevocable. People of faith have a fight in them that does not allow them to be comfortable with anything or any situation that is contrary to God's promise over their lives. People of faith refuse to stop expecting until they win.

Living by faith usually always involves a battle between what we see in front of us, and what we believe in our hearts. Every soldier knows that it is critical to have people in their trenches who are fully committed to fighting the cause with them, people who will provide support and fight with them till victory is declared and every insurgent destroyed. It is imperative that as we journey through life with faith, we surround ourselves with people who are fuelling our faith, rather than draining it. If those you see around you are not fueling you, you must be ready to separate yourself from them, in order to fight the fight of your life.

Faith also means being able to separate yourself from past negative experiences and still expect a positive outcome this time around. True faith will cause you to split away from people and surroundings that are not conducive to your growth and your walk of faith.

Maybe its time we separate!

Great ideas about faith...

'Faith makes the discords of the present the harmonies of the future.'
- ROBERT COLLYER

'The reason birds can fly and we can't is simply that they have perfect faith, for to have faith is to have wings.'
- JAMES MATTHEW BARRIE

'Whatever God's dream about man may be, it seems certain it cannot come true unless man cooperates.' - STELLA TERRILL MANN

'The prayer that reforms the sinner and heals the sick is an absolute faith that all things are possible to God - a spiritual understanding of Him, an unselfish love.' - MARY BAKER EDDY

My Thoughts

13

Faith Blockers

"For every child of God defeats this evil world, and we achieve this victory through our faith." 1 John 5:4 (NLT)

On this journey of faith, just like any journey in life, we can experience barriers, stumbling blocks, potholes and blockades that quench or diminish our faith, and our ability to fully be reliant on God. No one is exempt from experiencing moments of despair, desperation, discouragement, and those moments when we feel that we are all alone in our situation.

In the Bible, Moses, the same great man of faith, who we have come to know as a man who trusted God, who was chosen by God to lead the Israelites out of captivity experienced doubts. Being a person of strong faith does not mean you won't experience these type of moments, it is more to do with how swiftly you are able to pick yourself back up, dust yourself off and get back on the saddle of faith.

Faith blockers are those things, those emotions, those people, those situations that stop us from keeping our eyes on Christ and His promises. Anything that makes an attempt on you to stop you from believing God, that blocks your view of what God has planned for you, and makes you want to throw in the towel and quit, is a faith blocker.

At times, our faith blockers are self inflicted, whilst there are also times when we experience faith blocks due to external factors. Whether self inflicted, or whether caused by the weatherman or the traffic warden, or the devil itself (let's not humanise the devil, by calling the devil a 'him'. The devil is a 'it', a nasty 'it' that has no victory, and no authority over the life of a believer), a course of action is still required on our part to eradicate the faith blockers that are vying to discourage and distract you and I from entering into our promised land. Whenever we experience faith blockers, it is very difficult, almost impossible, at that moment to visualise God as being a personal, loving God, or that He is even remotely interested in our situation or our affairs.

Just like when you have vermin in your home, the first thing to do is search for the source or the point of entry. When we are vying to deal with and eradicate our faith blockers, it requires self-examination. It requires for us to take a deep, honest and no-holds barred review of ourselves, and the things we are allowing to feed on our mind, our spirit and also the status of our walk with God.

Here are some faith blockers that I have experienced in my own life and walk of faith:

A poor image of God

At times, we are so consumed with the magnitude of our mountains, that we develop a poor imagery of Who God is, and His unlimited abilities. Whenever we limit God, we start to experience moments of defeat, and self pity which then isolates us from God.

Sin

Sin causes us to be out of the presence of God. After sinning, Adam and Eve were cast out of the garden. Sin has a way of separating us from God, and when we become separated from God, we are not plugged in to the endless resources and encouragement associated with God. Sin causes us to feel ashamed, and takes away our ability to believe that God has great things and goodness awaiting us on the other side of our trials and tribulations.

Guilt

A by-product of sin, guilt is what the enemy wants us to experience. Romans 8, verse 1 tells us that 'there's no condemnation to those in Christ Jesus', guilt is something no believer should feel, because we know that all our sins have been forgiven, even those ones that are off the scales. The fact is that the Blood of Christ has pardoned us from every guilty verdict that sin caused, yet the enemy sows seeds of condemnation in our minds to make us feel that certain sins or life styles we indulged in are beyond the pardon of God. Guilt stops us from approaching God with confidence, it makes us feel unworthy of God's goodness.

Doubt

Doubt occurs whenever we develop an alternative to God's promises, and start to allow fear to creep in on us. Many of us doubt because we've either not truly experienced God's unlimited ability to come through for us, we've not truly meditated on His Words – which is God's CV, outlining His experience, abilities and skills. Or maybe we have simply become ignorant of what He did previously.

Lack of exposure to the Word

We grow by what we feed on. Whenever we starve ourselves from the Word or fail to allow ourselves to be exposed to the Word, we will not have enough fuel in the tank to journey through this highway of faith.

A poor self image

Having a poor self image is destructive. Many times we experience faith blockers because we do not feel that we are worthy enough to be blessed. We fail to see that we have been wonderfully and fearfully crafted by God. We see ourselves based on our failures and our negative experiences, rather than embracing the regeneration power of God, and expecting nothing but God's very best. We are clothed in the righteousness of Christ. This is what makes us worthy. A poor self image also causes us to see ourselves as inadequate. We must remember that in times of weakness and inadequacy, God's matchless strength is working in and through us. God has a knack for using unqualified people like you and me to accomplish great things. We need to take our eyes off ourselves and keep them on God. Humility and a poor self image are two different things. Humility says 'I can't do anything without God', a poor self image simply says, 'I can't do anything'.

Fear of failure

Oftentimes, we refuse to walk by faith or embark on a project that requires faith because we are concerned about the 'what if's!'; 'what if I fail?', 'what if He doesn't come through?', 'what if I don't get healed?' This is a major area of concern, and a greater blocker of faith for many of us. We lament and second guess God's ability, and start to process all the possible negative outcomes that could occur. God will never give you a vision or a promise and leave you all alone to work out the details. God is in the details. God is not a teaser; He doesn't give you a glimpse of what is possible, and then snatch it away from you. Stop allowing the possibility of failure to cripple you and overshadow the greater possibility of success.

Fear of success

It is rather easy to understand why someone could have a fear of failure, but oftentimes, we experience faith blocks because we are afraid of the success and the possibilities that comes with walking by faith. We are afraid because we've never been on the winning side of a battle, or we've never experienced abundance, therefore the impending unknown and the possibilities become scary. Many people are afraid to dream big or ask God for big things simply because they've become so accustomed to 'normal' and a 'just getting by', or even a poverty mentality that they would prefer not to exercise faith and merely just exist and float through life, than step into unchartered territories. Walking with God will take you places that will literally blow your mind and exceed your own limited human imagination. Some people are merely content to play if safe. Faith does not understand how to play it safe, and cannot accept being ruled by life's circumstances.

Once you've established the faith blockers in your life, make a non-negotiable commitment to be obedient to God always, and leave the consequences of your obedience to God.

The journey of faith is not an easy one. The road that faith causes us to walk in is never always smooth. It will have potholes and road humps, but with great tenacity, dedication and confidence in God, keep your foot on the accelerator and press on forward.

What blocks your faith? Attack it now!

Great ideas about faith...

'There are many things that are essential to arriving at true peace of mind, and one of the most important is faith, which cannot be acquired without prayer.' - JOHN WOODEN

'Love means to commit oneself without guarantee, to give oneself completely in the hope that our love will produce love in the loved person. Love is an act of faith, and whoever is of little faith is also of little love.' - ERICH FROMM

'No matter how steep the mountain, the Lord is going to climb it with you.' - HELEN STEINER RICE

'A faith of convenience is a hollow faith.' - FATHER MULCAHY

'The only limit to our realization of tomorrow will be our doubts of today. Let us move forward with strong and active faith.' - FRANKLIN D. ROOSEVELT

My Thoughts

14

Yes We Can!

"The things which are impossible with men are possible with God." – Luke 18:27 (NKJV)

Hope has a voice... You!

Wherever you were in the world, from the skyscrapers of Hong Kong, to the beaches of Australia; from the favelas of Rio, to the coast of Ghana, all over the world, it was hard to escape the historic events that happened in the United States on a cold November evening in 2008. More than just a historic turning point in American politics, but also an event that suggested to millions all over the world - "Yes We Can!"

Irrespective of our political affiliations, Barack Obama will go down in history, as having achieved a monumental feat as the first black president of the United States. However, the most important lesson here is what President Obama expressed throughout his campaign and subsequent election victory for - Hope is alive! Throughout his presidential campaign, and against all logical odds, Barack Obama spoke passionately about the concept of hope. A hope we can believe in, a hope that radiates in the lives of all human beings.

Hope is what allows and empowers each and everyone of us to wake up each morning, with great expectations; trusting and believing that "All things are possible!" Hope is the weapon we use against the critics, cynics, and naysayers of our dreams and God given visions. Hope is birthed when we partner with God, and He propels us to do great and awesome things; overcoming all odds and weathering every storm. Many of us feel overwhelmed with the troubles of life whenever we attempt to do big things, or whenever we are confronted by big mountains in our lives. This overwhelming feeling comes from attempting do things in our own strength and through our own limited thinking. When we are in partnership with God, we are strengthened in the fact that with God, we automatically become the majority. Therefore rather than being filled with dread, despair and discouragement, we are filled with an indestructible amount of confidence.

Apostle Paul reminds us that 'We can do all things through Christ, who strengthens us...' (Philippians 4:13) Our faith, and hope is not in our abilities, but in the One Who called us, Who gives us strength and Who purposed us before the foundation of the world. Knowing of our partnership with God gives us the wings to fly, and the keys to be set us free from every negativity, every limitation, every disappointment, every guilt, every setback and every critic. Yes We Can! It is time we start to dream again, expect again, because for those who are in Christ, and connected with Him, nothing is impossible!

What the enemy desires is for us to live below our potential, not to embrace the abundant life Jesus has for us, to give up on our dreams, to stop believing, to stop becoming, to throw in the towel, to quit when we are almost there! However, I strongly believe that through our faith in Christ, and the significance of John 10:10b "I have come, so that they might have life, and life more abundant", we have been given the liberty to say "Yes we can!"

I believe that because of God's divine partnership investment, inside of you is greatness, unlimited potential, the ability to heal from brokenness, the ability to fight against every temptation, the ability to overcome addictions, the ability to make inspired dreams a living reality and the ability to be a fruitful believer. Let us stop punching beneath our weight, limiting what God can achieve through us, and do for us. We have been created in His image, and we have been called to live a life of absolutely No Limitations! It is time to start embracing the change and possibilities that God can achieve through each of us, because 'the stone the builders have rejected, is now becoming the chief cornerstone...' (Matthew 21:42) God is bringing people from the gutters, the slums, the prisons, the dark alleys, the background, and promoting them to the forefront and setting them up for greatness.

God is like the coach in the corner of the ring, screaming to each of us – 'no matter what you've been through, and the circumstances you find yourself in. He is doing a new thing and YES YOU CAN!' In response and in obedience, we need to start believing what God, our divine Creator and Our Divine Partner thinks and says about us, and affirm daily - 'YES WE CAN! The 'We' denotes the fact that you are not in this battle alone; it's you and God – a truly awesome and unstoppable tag team.

Partnership with God gives us an advantage, places us in a vantage point. It enables us to get out of debt, be healed, be made over again, be restored, find peace, and live a victorious life.
Real faith is connecting with God, and staying connected with Him through all of life's ups and downs. Failure is rendered impossible when we partner with God, and give Him 'access all areas' in every area of our lives and daily living.

Great ideas about faith...

'I have held many things in my hands, and I have lost them all; but whatever I have placed in God's hands, that I still possess.'
- MARTIN LUTHER KING, JR.

'As your faith is strengthened you will find that there is no longer the need to have a sense of control, that things will flow as they will, and that you will flow with them, to your great delight and benefit.'
- EMMANUEL TENEY

'When walking through the "valley of shadows," remember, a shadow is cast by a Light.' - H. K. BARCLAY

'Child like faith focuses on our Heavenly Father - not on our fears.'
– ANONYMOUS

'Faith is not just something you have, it's something you do.'
– BARACK H OBAMA

My Thoughts

15

Faith Speaks

"Let no one despise your youth, but be an example to the believers in word, in conduct, in love, in spirit, in faith, in purity."
– 1 Timothy 4:12 (NKJV)

Can the real person of faith please stand up!

One of the most important things in life is for each of us to ensure that our character does not betray our talk. In essence, faith requires that we 'practice what we preach!' I've come across people who have expressed that they were too shy to talk about their faith, or the fact that they felt uncomfortable publically displaying their faith. I used to be like this also; I didn't want to be seen as an over-religious, in your face, bible bashing, party-pooper type of believer, who people cross over the road in order to avoid. Then I had a 'eureka moment'. A moment when I realised that faith is not simply just about what I tell people I believe; My faith is given a voice by the way I live each day, my lifestyle, my choices, and the way others see me react to life's ever changing scenarios.

I have come to realise that in life, numerous people can talk real good talks; they can brag about their accomplishments, their educational achievements, their dreams, their imaginary lifestyles, their goals and their ability to handle pressure. However, it is only in the midst of that pressure cooker, or when their talk is under the microscope called life, can they truly be tested to see who is truly who they say they are.

The most dynamic and most impactful way to express and share our faith is to allow our life, and our character to do all the talking, Talk can be very cheap. People are looking for those who's walk of faith is in alignment with who they say they are. The way we react, our level of expectations, our ability to stay calm even in the midst of pressure, our resolve, our ability to choose to see life through the lenses of faith, our ability to endure tough times, our ability to bounce back from life's setbacks and disappointments and our ability to encourage others even whilst we are facing our own personal challenges, shows the true nature of our faith.

In the corporate world, most recruiters I come across have highlighted the fact that when a new CV lands on their desk from a candidate listing all their attributes and achievements, and using words such as 'works well under pressure', 'adaptable', tenacious', 'hard worker', and even the old cliché - 'punctual', they are not swayed by the candidates long list of attributes. When I asked for their explanation to their dismissive approach, all mentioned that candidates often write down what they feel the recruiter wants to hear in order to get a job offer, without actually possessing those skills. Instead, they prefer to bring in the candidates to take part in a group assessment day, where recruiters aim to filter out those who truly possess the attributes on their CV, and those who just simply wrote down nice words.

Faith is like these. We are to live a life of faith, not just talk about a life of faith. Unfortunately, many people's brag about their faith is betrayed by their lack of faith when it truly matters.

Recently, I was in conversation with a family friend of ours who was going through the possibility of redundancy in her workplace. With a mortgage, a family, bills , expenses to think about, she could have allowed the looming redundancies to overwhelm her, and cause her panic. Rather, she would be the first one into the office every morning, she would encourage her work colleagues who have become so distraught by the possibility of their job security been taken away from them. This young lady, filled with faith still had an air of positivity around her, which caused others to have hope. This is exactly what faith does. When we as people of faith can still be faithful and be confident in God, irrespective of our circumstances, it liberates not only ourselves, but those around us. It empowers others to dream again, and to believe that the best is yet to come.

When we exercise faith, regardless of our environment and our current experience, we are shouting victory from the mountain top even before the battle is over. Faith, when exercised, acts as a lighthouse, which gives light to others who might be experiencing moments of darkness and despair in their lives. This confidence comes from knowing that our faith does not exist in the power of man, or is not determined by the strength of what opposes us, but rather in the power and limitless ability of God. Believing that no matter what, God's power will prevail gives us a peace that is unexplainable, but speaks through our actions and reactions.

Some people, when asked 'how are you doing?', will take a look at their circumstances, their home situation, bring the thought of the job they dislike into the front of their mind, will look at the English weather, think about their uncomfortable and annoying Tube journey to work, and automatically conclude that they are having a miserable day. Whereas, a true person of faith will simply think about God and His love for them, and conclude that life is beautiful. Irrespective of...! The glass is always half full for people of faith, and they are not ashamed to let the world see their glass on display.

People of faith are always excited about life, they always see the positives and the possibilities, even when the current climate and conditions are negative. Why? Because they know that at any moment, God can flip the script. They have an unwavering conviction that even if God decides not to flip the script, there is a lesson to be learnt, or a character trait within them that is being corrected.

True faith says that "there is never a hopeless situation, only people that stop hoping!"

What does your faith say about you?

Great ideas about faith...

"He who has faith has... an inward reservoir of courage, hope, confidence, calmness, and assuring trust that all will come out well - even though to the world it may appear to come out most badly."
- - B. C. FORBES

"Man, I just feel blessed... I was in a situation where the only way I could come out of it was by putting my faith in God. No matter how good my lawyers were, no matter how much celebrity I had, everything was just stacked up against me."
- SEAN 'P. DIDDY' COMBS

"Put your nose into the Bible everyday. It is your spiritual food. And then share it. Make a vow not to be a lukewarm Christian. "
- KIRK CAMERON

"Faith is the strength by which a shattered world shall emerge into the light." - HELEN KELLER

"All who call on God in true faith, earnestly from the heart, will certainly be heard, and will receive what they have asked and desired. " - - MARTIN LUTHER

My Thoughts

16

Semper Fidelis

'But let him ask in faith, without any doubting, for he who doubts is like a wave of the sea, driven by the wind and tossed.' – James 1:6

Semper Fidelis is the Latin word for 'Always Faithful'. The United States Marine Corps (USMC) adopted it as their motto in 1883, to signify the faithfulness, trust & dependence each marine has with his fellow marines. Marines promise to be faithful to the very end, even unto death; which goes as far as never leaving the body of their fallen comrades in a theatre of war (battle field). Rather, the marines would carry their fallen comrade's body on their shoulders, back to their base camp. With this in mind, the US Marine Corps live up to their motto.

For many of us who have never been in the US marines, it is good news to know that God's very own motto is Semper Fidelis. For Our God is always faithful!

As reiterated throughout the pages of this book, faith requires an object. We are to have faith in God and take Him at His word. Therefore, it is essential that the object which our faith is placed upon is faithful. God's characteristic of being a faithful and reliable God, enables us to be at peace even in the midst of the craziest of storms, because His faithfulness has been proven and His track record has no blemish.

We are called to have faith in a faithful God, a covenant keeping God, Who never turns away from His word & His promises. Many of us loose our faith when we experience the turmoil and storms of life. We begin to become discouraged by whatever life is throwing at us; we get caught up in all the uncertainties that surround us. Often times whenever we take an inventory of our life and the circumstances we find ourselves, and all we can see is the rubbles, derelict, brokenness, loneliness and emptiness of our current state, we begin to doubt God's faithfulness and His ability to keep His promise.

However, I have found that faithfulness is not about 'good times' only; Faithfulness says 'I'll be there through the good times, through the bad times and the ugliest of times...I'll always be there!' Coming to an understanding of what faithfulness truly is, allows us to take our eyes off the problem, and fix our attention on God, because He tells us that He will always be there to pull us through. True, genuine friendships & relationships are never proven during the jolly times, but rather through hard times, painful experiences and the times when we don't have any answers. However, God is always there, because He is always faithful. He promised 'never to leave us, nor forsake us...'

I have learnt not to be overwhelmed or downcast by life's many challenges and storms, because deep down in my Spirit and from previous encounters of God moving on my behalf, I know 'This too shall pass!' (Storms are only for a season), and as long as God is with me, then that's all I need to get through.

God did not promise us that troubles won't come our away, nor did He promise us that we would float through life without trials and potholes, so let us resist the temptation of constantly and unapologetically complaining to God about what He is taking us through and questioning His faithfulness. What we ought to do is conjure up an attitude of gratitude and victory, that enables us to start praising God for being present with us in the midst of our storms. The fact that God is with us, is a sure sign that our victory is a step closer. Praise and joyfulness are not things we should only experience at the end of the battle, but rather even in the midst of our troubles, because it shows that we truly understand and believe and have confidence in the faithfulness of God.

We are assured and reassured several times over in the Word that no matter what we go through in this life, God will give us a special type of peace that surpasses all understanding and all logic. The peace that comes from God is the kind that the world, doctors, scientist and atheists cannot comprehend. They look on the situations in our lives and wonder why we haven't come unglued, why we haven't thrown in the towel, why we haven't given up on God! But we know, that peace is not just the absence of problems, but it is knowing Who to look to when all hell breaks lose around us. This peace is knowing that every situation and every area of our lives are in God's competent & faithful hands. It is a matter of believing that the One to whom I have committed them has the answer, and that He has the power to change every situation for a positive outcome. Peace comes from utter trust in God, and His ability to bring us through. Personally, I have never been let down by God, and I am assured that He will never let me down! The reason is that God has always given me what I need, when I needed it. He might not have given me all I wanted, but I'm grateful that He supplies all my needs. It's our needs He promised to meet, not our wants, which are often born out of greed, jealousy and carnality.

The book of Lamentations is regarded by many as the saddest book in the Bible, because of its contents, and sorrowful tone. However, in the midst of the pain and sadness, is birthed the inspiration for one of the most famous hymns ever written 'Great is Thy Faithfulness.' This age old song is sang by believers and non-believers at weddings, funerals, birthdays, baby dedications all across the globe.

'I will never forget this awful time, as I grieve over my loss. Yet I still dare to hope, when I remember this: The faithful love of the LORD never ends! His mercies never cease. Great is His faithfulness; His mercies begin afresh each morning. I say to myself, "The LORD is my inheritance; therefore, I will hope in Him!" The LORD is good to those who depend on Him, to those who search for Him.'
- Lamentations 3:20-25 (NLT)

Please do not allow your faith to be moved by changing seasons and dark days, let our faith be solid as a rock, because God, Who is the object of our faith never changes, and He can do anything but fail. Understanding the faithful nature of God, affords each of us the ability to live a balanced life. A balanced life is one whereby we are able to take the hard hits of life, go through storms and yet still be able to rest confidently in God's ability to come through for us – just in time!

Hebrews 11, verse 6 talks of the fact that God rewards those who diligently seek Him. To diligently seek God means that you are sure that He is able to give you that which you seek Him for. God loves diligent seekers, because diligent seekers don't have an alternative plan, or an option B when it comes to where they source their help from. They know deep in their hearts 'its God or nothing!' Their faith in God's faithfulness cannot be deterred or diminished by situations or circumstances.

Even the great writer William Shakespeare referred to God's faithfulness as 'constant as the northern star'. True faith means that even when it seems or feels like God is not answering our requests, He is merely giving us the opportunity to grow and He is cooking up a tasty and finger-licking victory for us. Therefore true faith is not moved by God's apparent silence concerning our case; True faith is anchored on God's unwavering faithfulness, and can smell victory even in the midst of chaos. Can you smell what the Lord is cooking?

My God, is Semper Fidelis

Great ideas about faith...

'Prayer is the key to Heaven, but faith unlocks the door.'
– ANONYMOUS

'I know God will not give me anything I can't handle. I just wish He didn't trust me so much.' - MOTHER TERESA

'A better world shall emerge based on faith and understanding.'
- DOUGLASS MACARTHUR

'Hidden behind every difficulty is at least one opportunity and maybe more.' – A R BERNARD

My Thoughts

The "f" Word

Faith Inspirations

The following pages are a mixture of messages I have blogged over the years, and inspirational faith-nuggets that will hopefully fuel your faith.

Be inspired!

U Turns

A while back, I was driving on the South Circular (A205) in London, and came across an old church with a sign displaying the bold statement – 'God believes in U Turns!' When I saw this, it was a real blessing and reminded me that no matter how off track and how far off-course I have gone, there is a God who is ready to take me back into His embrace, if I make that choice. That choice to make a U Turn.

For those of us that drive, when we take a wrong turn or find ourselves travelling on the wrong road on our journey, we have 3 choices presented to us: get mad and tear our hair / weave out (rather expensive choice!); throw the cat out of the window and run over the lollipop lady (both of which are criminal offences in good ole' England); or we could continue on the wrong road and see where it eventually leads us. Or more simply we could check all traffic around us and make a U Turn to get back on track in order to reach our intended destination.

Family, the key thing here that I would like us to take note of is that oftentimes we do find ourselves off track, going away from our conscience, going away from the will of God, and trying to do things our own way. A few years ago, I had to face my own demons head on, and I had to re-evaluate my life and the road I was travelling on. It became clear to me that drugs, strip clubs, hedonistic sexual exploits and blood-stained Rolex watches were not the right way to live! I had to make a U Turn so I could get away from the things of the world which were leading to spiritual, emotional and physical death; turn back on myself and do a 180 degrees turnaround in order to get back on the road which leads to life, and back into the embrace of Christ. In other words, I GOT MYSELF TOGETHER!

Travelling on the road to nowhere is the most wasteful of human potential and human life. Travelling without purpose and without destiny in mind is a total waste of life; God's great investment in you and me is too precious and valuable to be wasted as such.

What's the great thing about U Turns? You can make a U Turn whenever and wherever you come to the realisation that there must be more to life than this (Current condition)! Just like the prodigal son who 'came to himself...' Family, God wants to do a new thing in our lives. He wants to give us joy, victory and favour in every area and facet of our lives. He wants to take something old and form something new...and that's you! That's what God did with Jacob, who was the trickster and the manipulating son of Isaac. He turned him around and gave him a new name and a new life as Israel.

"Forget about what's happened; don't keep going over old history. Be alert, be present. I'm about to do something brand-new. It's bursting out! Don't you see it? There it is! I'm making a road through the desert, rivers in the badlands." Isaiah 43:19 (The Message Bible).
"Therefore if any man be in Christ, he is a new creature: old things are passed away; behold, all things are become new." 2 Corinthians 5:17(King James Version).

I would like you to take a moment and search deep within, search out the areas of your life you are unhappy with, the habits that are holding you back from being all that God has created and formed you to be, and make that decision to make a U Turn! Get back in the embrace of God. It starts with a decision and a choice, which both belong to you: 'the ball is in your court.' God has already made His decision and His choice, which was to make a way out, to enable you and I to make a U Turn – Jesus on the cross

The great thing about that sign on that old church building was that the 'U' was written in large bold font, which I perceived denotes the truth that God doesn't only believe in U Turns, but ultimately God believes in U! Now, I want you to fathom enough faith to take the first step and make a U Turn...

God's Got Me Covered!

Probably the most important thing in our Christian walk, apart from knowing that Christ paid a price for us all on Calvary, therefore saving you and me from the clutches of the enemy, is to know that in all that we go through, God has you and me covered!

It gives us a real confidence in spite of all of life's threats, life's pressures, challenges, obstacles, and even in spite of the haters and naysayers that surround us; to know, and have the knowledge that God has us covered!

We are covered whenever we face a challenge or an uncertainty on our journey along the road of life, or simply when life just happens! When the issues and struggles of life seem to just weigh us down and we tend to feel alone, rejected and simply exhausted. When we get laid off from work (I believe the politically correct term, aka 'you can't sue us' terminology is 'down-sizing'), or it's the first day of the month and the bills still can't get paid and you feel like everything and everyone has been stripped away from you; this can lead to us throwing a pity party for ourselves rather than understanding that there is a purpose behind everything we encounter in this life, including every storm and every pain we may experience.

I believe in such circumstances that God is trying to get us focused on Him: He is using all these situations and pain to say to you &

I… "I have the whole world in My hands and I've got you covered!" In the Bible Paul reminds us of a great principle which can literally 'save our lives' and help us keep sane in an insane world. "And he said to me, 'My grace is sufficient for you: for my strength is made perfect in weakness…'" 2 Corinthians 12:9 (NIV)

God is trying to teach us to know, understand and walk in the knowledge that He is sufficient enough for all that we go through. In essence, He is all we need to survive! He wants us to know that. He knows what is happening to us better than we do, because His plans for us are of good and not evil, to give us a future and a hope! (Jeremiah 29:11)

God uses every struggle and every hardship of our lives not to destroy us but rather to challenge and prompt us to fully trust Him: to practice what we preach (because some of us can preach faith but we don't want to live by faith…ouch!), to draw closer to Him and rely solely on Him.

When we've exhausted all of our own ideas, plans, connections and options and we are now at breaking point, unable to see the light at the end of the tunnel or see a way out of our wilderness experience, that's when God can now step in and 'do His thing!' without any interference or 'help' from us.

In the current climate of economic failure, credit crunches, terrorist threats, the crumbling morality of our society, political uncertainties, job losses and family breakdowns, we find ourselves in a world on the verge of bursting under the pressure and strain of both natural disasters & spiritual threats which can leave us depleted and discouraged. Oftentimes it's difficult to watch the news or read the morning papers without a sense of discouragement coming over us. But nevertheless, despite the dangers, we as people of faith can live in a shaking world with an unshakeable confidence in the safety of His protection and His grace. We are reassured in Psalm 91:4 that.. "He shall cover you with His feathers and under His wings you shall take refuge" (New King James Version).

Family, as you go through the journey of life, through the junctions and twists and turns, whilst reaching out to the destiny that He has in store for you, remember God is using every opportunity to say to you "I've got you covered!... I'm enough for you! ... Just trust me!" In all that we experience, the good, bad and ugly episodes, God is covering us. Therefore, let us walk in confidence, in faith, and ultimately in victory!

But God!

Each of us have encountered or are currently going through situations where we just felt like giving up and throwing in the towel; we felt like the whole world was against us and no matter what we did, it never seemed to be enough.

We've found ourselves saying to ourselves, 'no matter what I do, things never seem to change, and I never seem to measure up'. We feel like we are in such a dark tunnel that there is 'no hope on earth' or 'no way out'.

This message takes its inspiration from the well known saying - "It's not over till the fat lady sings!"

For those of us who believe God, and who place the entirety of our hope in Christ no matter what challenges we come up against, we don't have to believe or feel that all hope is gone. We know that there is no such thing as a hopeless situation, and that is a fact! We believe that because we serve a risen Saviour, a loving Father, we can always face tomorrow, we can always live victorious lives!

All over the Bible, there are a number of powerful and explosive 2-word phrases, for example: 'Healed All' 'Cast Out' 'Raised Up' 'Pulled Down.' These words are used in the context of what God can and does do.

However, 'But God' – used forty three times in Scriptures surpasses them all, in my own child-like opinion.

'But God', is an exclamation and affirmation that should communicate a tremendous & heart warming message of hope to us all, whenever we hear or read it! For it is God's response to the enemy's challenge and the storms of life. It is the bottom line, it is the last word on every dilemma, situation and issue!

'But God', when looked at in relation to the challenges of our lives, is what YES is to NO! It's what LIFE is to DEATH. When the world tells you "No you can't", 'But God' replies "Yes I Can". When the critics say "you won't amount to anything" 'But God' says "You will be all that I have created you to be."

'But God' climbs the highest mountains, crosses the darkest valleys and sings a song of victory even in the midnight hour! 'But God' is courageous, it is confident and it is conclusive! 'But God' is about second chances, it's about having another go at what previously eluded you.

Too many times, we look at things through our own eyes and only see failure. 'But God' tells us to look at things, situations, ourselves, others, as God sees them! I want to encourage each of you to start looking at your life, your future, your situations as God sees them; no matter what the enemy says about your life and your situation, please respond with – "But God!"

My prayer and hope for you is that you will continue to block out the naysayers and critics of your destiny, those energy drainers, and start listening to what God is saying to you through His Word.

Seasons Change

Isn't it amazing, that for a few months in the year, we are in shorts, bikinis (ladies only), buying ice cream and watching cricket on freshly mowed lawns. Whilst for other months in the year, we are in overcoats, gloves and shivering as we rush to get out of those dark winter evenings.

Look around you now, how things have changed! The season has changed, and we expected it, because we know, as believers and non-believers that SEASONS DO CHANGE!

This is a principle that God laid down from the beginning of time. In Genesis 8:22 the Scripture reads "While the earth remains... seedtime and harvest (seasons) and cold and heat, and summer and winter, and day and night shall not cease." In our own personal lives and in our everyday living, one thing that we need to come to terms with which can ultimately determine whether we 'stay in the fight' or 'throw in the towel' is that fact that seasons do change!

Each of us has gone through or is presently going through a season that feels very much like winter. Whereby everything just appears dead, lifeless, hopeless, miserable, damp, cold and dark. I've personally gone through many winter seasons in my life and I know that it hurts; it can feel like the loneliest moments of life where all help and support just seems to disappear. Where one is unable to see any fruits in their personal and Christian life and the question that comes to one's mind is 'God, if You really love me, then why am I going through all this?' I've found myself asking that same question. Then God brings into my remembrance that 'seasons don't last always!' God allowing you and me to go through the winter seasons of life should really be an encouragement to us all, because 'going through' signifies and tells us that the winter season is not the final destination, it's just a terminal which we pass through on the way to our real destination! (Note - is it me, or does the word terminal and temporary have a similar resonance?)

Winter does not last forever; we need to remind ourselves of that fact. No matter how bad things get, no matter how cold and lonely life feels, let's be reminded that seasons do change and after winter comes the spring time where freshness and newness are the order of the day; where we are able to step into the new things that God has laid out for us. It's often said that people who give up the fight and throw in the towel in their walk of faith and give up on God are those who have not mastered the season's principle. These are those who have not understood the fact that everything, absolutely everything, is temporal. Seasons will always change and situations in life will always change; nothing is eternal except God!

God oftentimes allows difficult seasons in our lives in order to mature us, to mould us, to take away the pride in our lives and to get us totally reliant on Him, and Him alone! There are no short cuts to maturity; seasons are designed to mature us.

When we are faced with a difficult season in life and all hell seems to be breaking loose, that is the time we need to cleave unto God more than ever before and ask that He will give us the grace to go through the difficulties of the winter season and stay in the race long enough (endurance) to reap the harvest of the spring and summer seasons of life.

I'm encouraging you to stay in the fight. Seasons will change and what we need to do is to ensure that we are sticking close to the One Who never changes, Who's love for us never changes, Who loves us despite and in spite of our mess. God is forever faithful, and He will bring to pass all that He has promised you and me. God sees you in your winter seasons, He hears your cries, He sees every tear, and He sees your fears and anxieties. He knows that at times you feel like giving up and knows your pain. He knows the pressures that life is putting you under. But His word for you right now is... 'My darling child, hold on...seasons will change!' 2nd Corinthians 4:7-9 reminds us... "But we have this treasure in earthen vessels, that the excellence of the power may be of God and not of us. We are hard-pressed on every side, yet not crushed; we are perplexed, but not in despair; persecuted, but not forsaken; struck down, but not destroyed..." (NKJV)

I Spy with My Little Eye...

We all remember those days in the playground or in the car on those long journey, when in order to drown out the boredom we are experiencing someone shouts out... 'I spy with my little eye, something beginning with....' How innocent a game that was... but unfortunately a lot of us are still going through life looking at things with 'our little eyes...'

Faith requires us to look at things not with 'our little eyes', but through God's 'perfect eyes.'

Oftentimes, when we are faced with a challenge or a circumstance, the natural instinct is to view or perceive the current challenge or circumstance as overwhelming and insurmountable. This is the result of looking at our problems and dilemmas through our own little eyes. This then leads us to become prisoners of fear, who have abandoned the promises that God has laid out for us and the ability to see God as able.

I strongly believe that no matter what we are faced with or what we are going through, if we are able to start looking at things through God's eyes, we are able to be set free from the clutches of fear and insecurities. The Bible tells us "Do not worry about tomorrow, for tomorrow will bring worries of its own. Today's trouble is enough for today." Matthew 6: 34 (NLT) What God is trying to get through to us is that most of the worries and anxieties we are experiencing due to fear are caused by how we have chosen to see things and these things do not always materialize.

"Consider it a sheer gift, friends, when tests and challenges come at you from all sides. You know that under pressure, your faith-life is forced into the open and shows its true colors. So don't try to get out of anything prematurely. Let it do its work so you become mature and well-developed, not deficient in any way." James 1: 2-4 (The Message Bible) This powerful Scripture reminds us that with every trial a blessing comes attached. We need to see this! We need to see that whenever we are faced with some kind of upheaval, we are simply around the corner from our blessings and our breakthrough. Let's start seeing our trials and tribulations as nothing more than preparation for the next level that He has in store for us. We need to be able to see and realise that, with every door that is slammed shut in our face, it is merely an opportunity for God to open a new door which will take us to new dimensions of blessings.

When we see a situation and get fearful, it's because our human eyes are conditioned to look at 'what has happened before', whereas our spiritual eyes are all futuristic, all hope, all faith. Perceiving incorrectly and seeing things through natural eyes has caused many people to give up their purpose, their blessings, their dreams, their families and their peace. We need to understand that the way we see a thing or situation will determine our response to the thing and to the situation.

We cannot talk about perceptions, and how we view things, without looking at David. As a young man, we learn that David came up against Goliath, who the Bible literally depicts as a 'man mountain'.

Rather than getting all shook up, and running for cover, David was able to perceive that the 'man mountain' standing in front of him was no match for the God he served and was merely a stepping stone for him to reach his God-ordained destiny. It is good to note that in order to reach what God has for us, we have to conquer mountains. However, we are only able to conquer based on how we perceive the mountain. A famous saying states that 'we cannot conquer what we refuse to face'.

There are so many things that have risen and will rise up against us, attempting to distract, derail, and discourage us from reaching out to the things God has planned for us. We have to make the decision in our mind whether we will see them as mountains that cannot be conquered, or believe what Paul says in Philippians 4:13 "I can do all things through Christ, who strengthens me." Our victories do not come by our own strength, or the size of our biceps, or the number of academic qualifications we have collated. Our victories are based on seeing ourselves as victors, and seeing correctly that our God is bigger than any situation we might face

'So they spread this bad report about the land among the Israelites: "The land we travelled through and explored will devour anyone who goes to live there. All the people we saw were huge. We even saw giants there, the descendants of Anak. Next to them we felt like grasshoppers and that's what they thought, too!'" Numbers 13:32-33 (NLT). In the Old Testament, another scenario depicts a very negative and fearful way of looking at things and situations. Caleb sent out some scouts to spy out the land and they came back with such a distressing report of themselves and made the situation 'un-winnable!' This report caused outrage and got people literally 'tearing out their weave.' In the following chapter, God was angry because He said to Moses '"How long will these people treat me with contempt? Will they never believe me, even after all the miraculous signs I have done among them?'" Numbers 14: 11 (NLT)

God desires for us to see Him at work on our behalf in every situation. God's plan for us is to see everything - every circumstance, every issue, every test and trial, through His perfect eyes because He has already seen the end from the beginning and He knows that everything will always work in our favour (Romans 8:28).

Let us engrave this fact inside us; that we have to see every situation we face through the eyes of Almighty God, because our human eyes are just too little to perceive correctly. Put on those spiritual glasses and let God filter out every fear, every anxiety and every doubt... YOU WILL WIN!

God Never Fails

On this journey of life, as we navigate through the ups and downs, the twists and turns and as we make every attempt to hold onto God's promises and His Word, we often get to a place whereby we start to debate whether God can actually see or even hear us. We find it that little bit harder to walk by faith and live in hope. I've been there too! I almost gave up and parked up right there too. But then something dawned on me which empowered me to put the car back in 'drive' and keep on moving - it was the sincere, unchangeable and unquestionable fact that GOD NEVER FAILS, simply because, He cannot fail!

When life hits us with its best shots and we don't feel that our season is changing for good, or we are experiencing negativity and defeat on every side, we often feel that God has failed us and He must be busy doing something for someone else. This is what the enemy wants you and I to believe, but how many of us know that the devil is a liar? I do! That's why I never trust my feelings, because feelings change, but fact is fact! Fact is a constant that never changes. Even when we do not feel that God is moving on our behalf or working things out for us, I like to believe that we have enough fact (The Word) to ensure that we can drown out those little voices that say 'God has abandoned you and will not keep His promises.' John 8:32 tells us '...you will know the truth, and the truth will set you free..." (NIV). The truth is what sets us free. Free from every unbelief, free from every feeling of abandonment, free from every doubt, free from every insecurity, free from every fear.

The old timers used to tell us 'delay is not denial!' There is so much truth in that statement because we often lose faith when we 'feel' that God is taking too long to bless us or give us the breakthrough that our current situation requires. The truth of the matter is that God's promises have an appointed time which is not often known to us; but be assured that His Promises will come to pass. We need enough faith to keep hoping, to keep trusting, to keep expecting, to keep pushing. The Bible tells us that 'Hope never disappoints!'

It is always a safe bet to trust God! He never fails because He cannot ever fail. He is God! The book of Proverbs tells us, "Trust in the Lord with all your heart; and lean not on your own understanding. In all your ways acknowledge Him, and He shall direct your paths." Proverbs 3:5-6 (NKJV).

As you read this message, please take a moment to think about all the things you're expecting God for and the situations you're waiting for God's intervention in, and the miracles you're expecting Him to perform in your life. Now in faith concerning those things and those situations, say "My God is able, He never fails, because He cannot fail!" In every area of your life, I encourage you to continue to trust God and stop listening to those little voices and start believing the BIG God! He will never fail you. Ensure you get (on a daily basis) some quality Faith Food to feed your faith and quench your doubts. Study the Word of God, get yourself into a faith building and Bible living Church, surround yourself with friends that will pray for you and encourage you in your faith walk because "...faith comes by hearing, and hearing by the Word of God' Romans 10:17 (NKJV). As you wait on God, your strength will be renewed and your hope restored. God will never fail you, keep on trusting.

My question to you is... do you believe that God will come through for you? I do!

"Some trust in chariots, and some in horses: but we trust in the name of the LORD our God." Psalm 20:7 (NIV)

I believe that God can and will do what He said He will concerning you, irrespective of how long He takes. We work on different time zones... God is not limited by chronos (time); He is from everlasting to everlasting - The eternal God!

I Am Not Forgotten...

There is probably nothing worse in this life than the feeling of being abandoned, neglected or forgotten about. We have all felt the heartache and pain when someone who told us they would call back never return our calls or replies our emails. We feel neglected, abandoned and alone. It appears the other person has forgotten about us...and we say to ourselves 'I must not matter after all...'

Many of us in life have felt abandoned by a loved one, our family members, the church, or by a person whom we gave our trust to, someone we were counting on. We then start to question ourselves, question our own self worth, doubt our identity, and start to focus on the negatives in our lives because we feel that we were abandoned because the other person discovered our flaws and ran a mile. Oftentimes, when we are going though life's struggles and trials and we are unable to envision a way out, we feel trapped and feel that even God has forgotten. When we cry ourselves to sleep at night and wake up with our pillows soaked in tears, we often wonder if God sees our tears, if He understands our pain, if He even cares! "Where is God when I needed Him the most?"

I often find myself comforting others or encouraging myself through the phrase 'There is a purpose in every pain...' which allows me to understand and truly trust that even in the midst of my pain, God still cares, because He promised me the Holy Spirit as a comforter –

to comfort me when the season is uncomfortable, when the sun fails to shine, when the tears keep on running.

It goes without saying that life sometimes hurts! It is unavoidable. We must all experience both the tears and joys of life; bad things do happen to good and faithful people. We must all go through pain, because even Jesus (God's very Own Son, God in human form) had to endure betrayal, torture, hurt and pain. Jesus asked The Father 'Why have thou forsaken me?...', but His thoughts then turned to the bigger picture, the bigger plan. There is purpose in the pain we endure in life, and when God allows us to go through it, it does not mean He has forgotten. Some things in life have to come to pass, as part of the bigger picture.

Whenever I see the homeless, the orphaned children as a result of war or disease, the helpless, the broken-hearted, the widowed, the down & outs...my heart bleeds and I cannot help but shed a tear. This is exactly how God feels; He counts the tears that roll down our cheeks. He sends us a comforting Word, a person to bring us a smile, a song in the midnight hour, a soft breeze through the trees, a rainbow after the rain; something to give us the strength to get through, which tells me that God never forgets. Pain is part of life, but having Jesus as your personal Lord & Saviour soothes the pain – that's why He is the Balm of Gilead – He takes the pain away - in due time.

Have I felt abandoned by God before? Oh yes! But He always brings me something to remind me that 'He will never leave me, nor forsake (abandon) me...' Hebrews 13:5.

The Psalmist Israel Houghton depicted this notion excellently in one of his songs: *'God knows my name, He is the father to the fatherless, He is a friend to the friendless, He gives hope to the hopeless, He mends the broken, He heals the sick, He gives strength to those who cannot help themselves...'*

Whatever you and I are facing right about now, we need to remind ourselves that there is purpose in every pain! God sees each tear that falls, He hears us even when we have no strength to speak out, He understands our groaning and moans. Even our tears have a voice that only God hears. He sees the abandoned young woman with the child, He sees the man that's just been laid off work, He sees those in the prison cells, those in the hospital bed, those whom life has been hard on, those who have been abused, He sees us all.
Not only does God see us, but He knows our names, and according to the Bible, He knows every strand of hair on our heads! We might feel lonely at times but we are definitely not alone! We might feel neglected and abandoned at times but I've learnt not to rely too much on feelings. It's better off for me if I just keep on trusting God's Words, knowing that even through the pain and heartache and hurt, God has given me the Holy Spirit to bring me comfort when life feels uncomfortable. Truly, I am not forgotten...

"He calls his own sheep by name and leads them out." John 10:3b (NIV)

Keep the faith...

Finger Licking Good!

Our God is truly a great and awesome God. It might not sound biblical or spiritual, but God truly rocks! He has a way of showing up when we need Him the most; He has a way of fixing things on our behalf. God ultimately has a way of reassuring us even in the bleakest, darkest, loneliest and most challenging times in our lives that He has our back! It takes me back to that old Sunday school song – 'He's got the whole world in His hands...'

Let's take a quick nugget out from the 23rd Psalm of the Bible. This must be one of the most personal, inspirational, and most memorised Scriptures penned in the Holy Bible. The 23rd Psalm kicks off with Who God is in terms of our relationship with Him. He is Our Shepherd. Whenever a sheep is in the presence of his or her Shepherd, the sheep is at ease knowing that irrespective of external 'going-ons' there will be no lack and no chance of any fox or wolf getting too close. A Shepherd is a provider, a guide, a protector, a healer. With the Shepherd in close proximity there is constant peace, which is refreshing to a soul. David was so eloquent and descriptive of the kind of peace that comes with being in God's presence by using the analogy of 'still water': that is the best description I know of a peaceful situation.

Even when we are challenged and oppressed or facing a situation that makes absolutely no sense, we are to 'fear no evil', for God is backing us up. He is with us, which is the highest level of comfort. Wow! God's presence allows and enables us to be comfortable even whilst our condition and environment are extremely uncomfortable.

For those of us who are surrounded by doubters, energy-drainers and pessimistic people, people who are unable to see the potential and the gift God has placed in us, well, God is gearing us up and setting us up for a feast, a fiesta, a celebration dinner with those same doubters and critics in attendance looking on. I can almost taste what God has in store, so much so that I can lick my fingers even now, as I await my breakthrough. How about you? Yummy! When our season comes, it will be a finger licking good moment, because God will show us off so that He can get the glory!

My urge to you today is to ensure that you stick with God and remain in His presence so that you can experience the peace, comfort, assurance, love, and finger licking good moments that only He – The Shepherd, can give. This is more than a KFC family bucket meal; this is eternal life. It's spending eternity with Him and experiencing His full goodness right here on earth, because we are His sons & daughters.

Man in the Mirror

"I'm looking at the man in the mirror...oh yeah!"

What sounds like an old Michael Jackson song truly echoes what the Bible says, in that we are to 'check ourselves out.' Oftentimes when things don't seem to be happening for us, or going our way, the first thing we tend to do is either put blame on external forces or make every attempt to alter and change the external factors. However, at times, we need to take a closer look at ourselves! Oftentimes in life, before we can change the outside, we must ensure that we clean up and fix up what is on the inside; then whatever change occurs on the inside will surely flow out to the outside.

One of the greatest inventions of all time would have to be the mirror. Here we have a very interesting, unique yet simple invention, which is able to reflect an image that is identical to the person or object in front of it. A mirror will only show and reflect what is placed in front of it.

'But be doers of the word, and not hearers only, deceiving yourselves. For if anyone is a hearer of the word and not a doer, he is like a man observing his natural face in a mirror; for he observes himself, goes away, and immediately forgets what kind of man he was. But he who looks into the perfect law of liberty and continues in it, and is not a forgetful hearer but a doer of the work, this one will be blessed in what he does.' James 1:22-25 (NKJV)).

The question remains: when we see our mess in the mirror, are we prepared to make the necessary change(s)? We would in the natural, so let us also do the same when it comes to our spiritual nature.

When we think about a mirror, four things come into play -

Individuality

When we look in the mirror, we will see no one else but ourselves. Oftentimes, we allocate too much time and effort looking at others, when in truth we should be looking at ourselves. This is a great thing about the mirror, because no matter how hard we try to look for someone else, maybe to possibly pass the blame onto, we will only ever see ourselves.

Revelation

When we stand in front of a mirror, it shows us things about our personal appearance that would otherwise be unnoticeable to us. The mirror gives us a way of checking ourselves.

Essential

Mirrors are essentials. Let's imagine how we might look in the mornings on our way to work, or in the evenings on our way out to a date or a dinner function, if we didn't take time to stop and see what the mirror sees. 99% of us would never leave home without checking ourselves out in front of the mirror. Even us men!

Reality

Mirrors cannot create an image; they can only reveal that which already exists. The mirror has no power or ability within itself to correct, change, or make alterations to what it sees. Only you, standing in front of the mirror, can change or make alterations to what you see.

I strongly believe that God's Word is our mirror. We need to daily check ourselves using it as our mirror and see if we as individuals and even the Church reflect God in our everyday lives. The Word is the standard that we check and measure ourselves against.

"For the word of God is living and powerful, and sharper than any two-edged sword, piercing even to the division of soul and spirit, and of joints and marrow, and is a discerner of the thoughts and intents of the heart. And there is no creature hidden from His sight, but all things are naked and open to the eyes of Him to Whom we must give account." Hebrews 4:12 –13 (NKJ)

Do you see something you don't like in the mirror? Well, choose to change it!

Don't Look Back in Anger!

How many times have you heard a person say to someone going through a trial, or maybe even had it said it to you when you've suffered a loss or experienced some kind of great tragedy or turmoil in your life - "I know it's difficult for you right now, but it's for the best!" Usually at the time when these words are being spoken to us they provide little if any comfort. Usually, we are thinking quietly in our minds, "It's easy for you to say. You have no idea what I am going through. You wouldn't say that if it were you in my shoes."

Although people's words at the time provide very little comfort, the Bible does teach us that everything that happens in the life of a believer (the good, the bad and the ugly things of this life), have an ultimately positive purpose. All we need to do is look at the life of Joseph to find an illustration of where we see bad things happening to a good man for the purpose of preparing and positioning him to be blessed and to be a blessing to others. His own brothers sold him into slavery. He finds himself in a pit, then a prison before being promoted to the palace. Even in the future, when he meets his brothers again, he was able to forgive, because he knew that what his brothers meant for evil, God was able to turn around for good (Genesis 50:22).

In the blockbuster film, Slumdog Millionaire, the lead actor was able to use all his negative experiences from his youth to be victorious on a game show. Rather than feeling sorry for himself and being angry, he was able to let go and turn those same negativities into positives. The Master Designer of our lives knows how our life will pan out. He has nothing but good and grandeous intentions for us. His thoughts towards us are of good and not evil. He promised that all things (both the positives & negatives) are working together for our good (positive!) Whatever we go through, God is still in control. We just need to get close enough to Him, rely on Him and trust Him, in order to see the bigger and brighter picture.

Things might appear and feel real hard and difficult right now, memories of your past might appear very bleak and negative, people might have met you with negativity, pushed you down, abused you, misused you, mistreated you, let you down, back-tracked on their promises to you, taken advantage of you and mistaken your meekness for weakness; but God is fighting for you and you too should look back at all you've been put through and say "You intended it for evil, but God turned it around for good...Look at me now, I'm still standing!"

For that reason, just like the old Oasis pop hit – 'Don't look back in anger!' God is turning your negativity into positivity; remember, the cross is a positive sign!

Keep the Change

Whenever we go on a shopping experience, whether it be for milk, bread, petrol or shoes, we engage in a transaction or an exchange - cash for goods. After every transaction, what we have left is the change. The same is also true for every experience in life; every experience and every circumstance that life takes us through always leaves a deposit; a deposit that will either make us or break us.

Life is full of twists and turns. At every stage and every turn in life, it is an opportunity to experience, to learn, to grow, to choose, to change. Whatever life takes us through, whatever hand we are dealt with, whatever disappointments, pain or hurt we've been dragged through, let us always use the experience. I strongly believe that absolutely no experience is a waste, nor should we choose to distance ourselves from what we've been through, no matter how negative we perceive it to be, because from it we learn; we learn who we really are, what we are made of and Who's we are (after all is said and done, Who we really belong to; The One who promises never to leave us, nor forsake us (Hebrews 13:5)). From the experience we also get to alter our perspective as we start to see the bigger picture, start to see God's perfect plan even in the midst of the chaos, and know that "all things are working together for our good..."

Whatever it might be, let's start disposing of the guilt, getting rid of the sense of hopelessness, letting go of the hurt, and deleting the 'I just got burnt' feeling or thinking; but keep the change!

Keeping the change will allow you in the future to look back on what the Lord has taken you through and where He has brought you from, and your faith will be strengthened by the knowledge that you've made it through before and therefore you can make it through again!

Personally, I have experienced countless events that have left me frustrated; events that have left me feeling hopeless and hurt. These events have caused me to cry out to God many times asking "Why?" and "When will this ever end?" At times it feels like I've received no answer to my moaning. But then, a feeling of comfort and peace comes over me which lets me know that God knows the future; He knows who I am and He has my best interests at heart. He knows how these experiences, good and bad, will help shape the way I am. I've realized this with a few things I've gone through in the past; my experiences have helped me when it comes to talking to and understanding people and the struggles we all face in this thing called 'life'. My experiences have made me stronger in many regards and have made me wiser to newer struggles so I don't have to fight my way through like I have in the past. I have also learned to trust and believe that whatever comes my way, God is in control and is using the actions of others and external factors to help me better myself and prepare me for things to come.

So when we are confused about a situation or angry that things aren't going our way, we can look to Him for strength, comfort and guidance, and trust in His promise that He will never leave nor forsake us. Just like Joseph in the Bible, we too can proclaim that "what man intended for evil, God has turned around for good."

Remember the saying 'If it doesn't kill you, it will make you stronger?' Well, that is so true, because you'll become stronger, wiser, so much better for the experiences and the situations that you have been taken through. Therefore family, no more bitterness, no more tears, no more sorrow, no more pity parties; it's time to start rejoicing and shouting from the rooftop, because God is working things out in your favour!

Whatever you do and go through, remember to always keep the change!

Humpty Dumpty

"Humpty Dumpty sat on a wall
Humpty Dumpty had a great fall
All the king's horses and all the king's men
Couldn't put Humpty together again...."

We are all familiar with this old school nursery rhyme; but have we ever related Humpty Dumpty to ourselves, or the situations we often find ourselves in?

Some of us can get up easily when we fall, but for some of us at times there are some falls which leave us shattered, battered, bruised and exhausted! Some of us are secretly still 'walking wounded' from a great 'fallen' experience; internally hoping that no one will realise that we have fallen and are broken! (side note: I am praying that very soon, we will be able to experience church where we can come as BROKEN as we are, without the need to hide our scars! Without the religiously correct need to 'act saved', or pretend that we are 'doing just fine', 'blessed & highly favored.' Let the truth be told – 'I'm fallen'... 'I'm slipping and I can't get up!')

I'm not sure about you, but when I first came to the Lord, I did not come to the Lord to fill a church pew or become a preacher or to become 'PG'; nor was it to travel the world to spread the Gospel or write books. To be truly honest, I had a selfish motive. I came to the Lord because I realised that I had fallen, I was broken, I was naked; everything that I had held in high regards had fallen from underneath my feet. I was broken in pieces, I was alone, unable to piece together the mess of my life, I felt stuck in a mud pit;

overwhelmed with guilt, choked by bad choices, unable to dream, unable to see any light at the end of the tunnel, unable to wake up from the nightmare which had become my reality. I came to God because I was desperate for someone who was willing and able to put back my broken pieces.

Some of us were lucky enough to be born into church & Christianity, surrounded with love & protection; but for some of us, we found ourselves like the prodigal son, 'in a far country...' In a fallen state, we came to God out of desperation! In need of direction, in need of hope, in need of a new lease of life, in need of a Saviour Who was able to put back the broken and shattered pieces of our lives!

Ever allowed a 'J Holiday' that was not your wife or husband to 'put you to bed?' Then you got up out of the wrong bed and a sense of guilt and brokenness crept up on you? Well, that's a fallen state...

Whenever we get out of position or 'dis-align' ourselves from God, or God's plans for our lives, that is a fallen state!

Family, have you found yourself in a fallen state?

Are you experiencing broken dreams? Broken promises? A broken life? A broken faith? God can, and He will, put you back together! That's what it says on His CV - "The Spirit of the Lord is upon me, because he hath anointed me to preach the gospel to the poor; he hath sent me to heal the brokenhearted, to preach deliverance to the captives, and recovering of sight to the blind, to set at liberty them that are bruised..." Luke 4:18 (NKJV).

If you feel broken, please do not turn to the world (all the king's horses and all the king's men) or try to fix yourself up before coming to God; He wants you to come to Him as broken as you are. He requires nothing from you apart from you surrendering yourself to Him so that He can make you whole again.

I often like to refer to God as the Potter, as symbolized in the book of Jeremiah. God is a potter, who is sitting at the wheel, with the clay (you and me) in His hands, and He has the ability to turn a broken clay pot into a vessel of honour, of greatness, because as long as we remain in the hands of the potter, He can fix us up and make us whole again!

So the rhyme should now read...

"Humpty Dumpty sat on a wall
Humpty Dumpty had a great fall
All the king's horses and all the king's men
Couldn't put Humpty together again....(The devil is a liar!)....
But Jesus came, paid the price, and made Humpty Dumpty whole again..."

Family, I am unsure of what you are dealing with privately; those things that you will not talk about, secretly hoping they'll just 'go away!' However, I do know that when life happens to us, it can leave us broken and exhausted, so exhausted that we become sick and tired of being sick and tired! But, let me tell you that from my own personal experience, even when people, friends and family cannot (or will not!) help you get back on your feet after a fall, God can (and will), because of these two passages: "But Jesus beheld them, and said unto them, With men this is impossible; but with God all things are possible." Matthew 19:26 (KJV)

"...His strength is made perfect in our weakness..."
2 Corinthians 12:9 (NKJV)

In Conclusion... Be Relentless

It is time to take your faith to a whole-nother level, believing God in the midst of all of life's turbulences. We began the journey of this book on a plane, and we shall visit a plane in concluding these pages. On a plane journey, we place our total trust in a Pilot whom we have no relationship with, and no prior knowledge of; yet we are confident in him or her to fly us to our desired destination in one piece. I strongly believe that we ought to place greater faith in God, and trust His Words above all else.

One evening I stumbled on a newspaper article on the story of people around the world who had overcome great adversities. The journalist listed a number of factors that was common to these people, and prevalent in all their stories. At the top of the list was the ability to be relentless.

Your faith must consistently be relentless. You must possess relentless faith in order to consistently be a victor, as oppose to a victim in this thing called life. Relentless faith is the breed of faith that resists the temptation to throw in the towel, and refuses to concede to current circumstances. A faith that is relentless looks to God's Word for the answers to all of life's dilemmas and challenges.

As you put your faith into practice, and you take those steps on the road to destiny; I urge you to be relentless in your pursuit of God; placing your total faith in Him. Relentless faith is unshakable, unmovable and unstoppable.

Successful people are those who possess the ability to see beyond the now; and are relentless in their belief of what is possible.

My prayer

That you will grow in faith and uncover all the blessings that God has for you. That you also discover that a life of true joy is experienced by being in a relationship with God, and placing your faith in Him, as you journey with Him through life.

To your success!
G AJEWOLE

About the Author

Inspirational Speaker | Pastor | Life Coach | Faith Builder | Author

Gbenga 'G' Ajewole, also commonly known as 'Pastor G', is fast becoming one of the UK's leading Ministers of the Gospel of Christ and an inspirational speaker. He has a genuine passion and desire to see people 'become all they were created to become' through his inspirational, thought-provoking, and witty messages.

Born in Akure, Nigeria, G moved to the UK at the age of nine. Growing up in South London, G learnt many life lessons at a tender age, and felt the effects of bad decisions and negative influences. In the autumn of 2001, G fully committed his life to Christ, and has since been on a quest to see lives transformed, potential unleashed and extend the loving grace of Jesus Christ that he experienced, to others.

G is a Business Administration & International Marketing (BA Hons) graduate, and previously worked for a number of Marketing and New Business Development agencies, before taking on the call of full time ministry.

A sought after youth speaker, G spent over five years as an itinerary youth speaker, speaking at churches, youth conferences, youth retreats, universities and prisons across the UK.

What makes G more special is his ability to motivate, inspire, engage and challenge individuals. He has been classified as a 'relevant preacher and speaker', who is able to take his listeners, whether it be in the church pews, or in school assemblies, on an inspired and transformational journey from their current reality to their ideal destination. G is truly a tool in God's hands for this generation. His ability to show vulnerability, and talk about his past, has been said to liberate many who are struggling with insecurity, addiction, guilt and a lack of faith.

G is married with a son. He resides in Kent, England (UK) with his family. He is the Lead Pastor of a dynamic church – Destiny Christian Fellowship (DCF) in London. He is also the co-founder of SAGE Ministries – a London based teens & young-adults ministry.

G Ajewole is sure to be an impactful, influential and unforgettable presence in the 21st century.

G is available to speak at schools, universities, churches, conferences, relationship seminars, and retreats.

To book G for your next event, please send email enquiries to info@inspired4purpose.co.uk